Shaping the Man Inside
TEENAGE BOYS!

Surviving & Enjoying
These Extraordinary Years

BILL BEAUSAY

WATERBROOK
PRESS

Teenage Boys!

All Scripture quotations, unless otherwise indicated, are taken from the Holy Bible, New International Version®. NIV®. Copyright © 1973, 1978, 1984 by International Bible Society. Used by permission of Zondervan Publishing House. All rights reserved. Scripture quotations marked (NKJV) are taken from the New King James Version. Copyright © 1982 by Thomas Nelson, Inc. Used by permission. All rights reserved. Scripture quotations marked (NLT) are taken from the Holy Bible, New Living Translation, copyright © 1996. Used by permission of Tyndale House Publishers, Inc., Wheaton, Illinois 60189. All rights reserved. Scripture quotations marked (NASB) are taken from the New American Standard Bible® (NASB). © Copyright The Lockman Foundation 1960, 1962, 1963, 1968, 1971, 1972, 1973, 1975, 1977. Used by permission. (www.Lockman.org)

Trade Paperback ISBN 978-1-57856-042-4
eBook ISBN 978-0-307-78958-7

Published in the United States by WaterBrook, an imprint of the Crown Publishing Group, a division of Penguin Random House LLC, New York.

WATERBROOK® and its deer colophon are registered trademarks of Penguin Random House LLC.

Printed in the United States of America
2017

25 24 23

Contents

Acknowledgments

I would like to express my sincere thanks to several people who have made this expanded version of *Teenage Boys!* possible. First to Dan Rich, president and publisher of WaterBrook Press, for his faith in me as a writer and for his undying passion to create books that matter.

I'd also like to thank the entire editorial staff and marketing team at WaterBrook. Special thanks to Ron Lee for his invaluable help in focusing my feeble ideas into a coherent bolt of intelligence in part 5 of this book; to Doug Gabbert, a father of the highest caliber and passionate salesman for this book; and Rebecca Price, the first person to look at my "stuff" and give me a shot.

No word of thanks would be complete without tipping my hat to my agent, Sara Fortenberry. Her expert and steady guidance through troubled times has meant the world to me. And of course my kids: Jake, Jessie, and Zac. You'll never know what you've allowed me to learn. I love you more than I can say. To Milane and Bill Beausay, my folks. You know what you mean to me. I love you both dearly.

To the countless people who have endured my seminars, allowed me to try out ideas and approaches, who witnessed me stumble and fall yet listened intently, I say thank you. You've allowed me to learn so much. You've made me think and create. My deepest prayer is that something in these pages will strike you as familiar, and you can know that you had a part in changing the world.

Introduction

You might think it's a little audacious for me to suggest we parents can actually survive and enjoy our children's teenage years. But it's true. I've proved it in my own family and seen it lived out in scores of others.

Personally, when I think about teenagers, I feel a fresh breeze in my heart. Why? With every piece of boyhood our sons put down, they're picking up another exciting possibility for adulthood. Another surprise. Another beginning. And God made you and me, as their parents, to succeed in our roles in this amazing process. Yes, we can shape the man inside the boy!

My premise in this book is straightforward: Our teenage sons are remarkable young men, and what we're watching unfold before us is nothing short of a miracle—their births as men. But it's a miracle we're meant to be part of. By using a lot of common sense and some powerful strategies I call provocative parenting, we can become influencers, encouragers, shapers, and inspirations. And have a lot more fun in the process.

The ideas you'll encounter here are drawn from my experiences as a professional counselor, consultant to world-class athletes, personal development product designer, and parenting teacher. But the source that excites me the most is the teenagers themselves. I've spent hours working and playing with, listening to and—I'll admit—shaking my head at some of the best. Two of them, Jake and Zac, call me Dad.

When it comes to mastering the parenting of teenage boys, big ideas just don't substitute for raw experience. In fact, you'll discover that my favorite problem-solving tool isn't all that sophisticated: Dive in! Anyone with teens in the house will find this book most helpful if they just attack this job with enthusiasm.

To that end, let me pray with you an extraordinary prayer I often share with parents of teens. It's by Brennan Manning:

May all your expectations be frustrated;
may all your plans be thwarted;
may all your desires be withered into nothingness...
that you may experience the powerlessness
and poverty of a child;
and sing and dance in the poverty of God;
Who is the Father, Son, and Spirit. Amen.

PART ONE

A Parenting Plan for Man-Making

Chapter One

Mission Possible

You can raise your teenage son successfully—and enjoy it!

If you picked up this book, chances are you're a little disoriented. Suddenly your baby boy is pushing six feet, and when he answers the phone, he sounds like Rambo. He's often quiet and withdrawn. Sometimes he seems angry or moody for no reason. He often mis-interprets your intentions and acts like your input is a contagious disease. And you're supposed to parent this kid for several more years? What began as a quest to build an extraordinary man may seem today like it's turned into the trail of tears!

I've got good news: The teen years can be some of the best in all of life for both you and your son. In the huge majority of cases, a parent can expect to raise a great teenage son and really enjoy it!

Many of us have been told so often of the horror of teenhood that we've become convinced it's true. I know. As I've spoken with friends and acquaintances about this book project, their reactions have been nearly identical: "You're gonna write a book about teenage boys? Ha! Are you gonna include duct tape and handcuffs?"

Unfortunately, what we believe about teenagers determines how we treat them. If we expect and wait for the worst, too often the worst happens. A change in thinking is overdue.

The early teenage years, especially those early adolescent years, are pivotal. Consider your own teen years for a moment. You established and perfected (for better or worse) a vast array of habits during that brief flicker of time. You decided which moral track to follow. You decided whether you would succeed or fail, be happy or sad, live life victoriously or tragically, and so on. Only now can you see in hindsight how those habits and actions shaped your life and how crucial some decisions were.

With these experiences beauty-marking (or pockmarking) our lives, occasional despair or fear for our teens is normal. We've invested an enormous amount of love, time, and personal attention in them, and we're extra concerned about their lives working out well.

This is all complicated by a God-breathed urge we parents feel to connect with our kids at all costs. We get frantic if we lose touch with them, and this can press us into desperate action. Or into dumbfounded passivity. We aren't dealing with children anymore. All the rules have changed, and we may not be sure where to turn.

Discovering how to meet these challenges, though not obvious, is easy.

You're thinking, *Easy? He doesn't know my kid!*

When I say easy, I mean there are some straightforward steps you can take to have immediate impact on your teenager. And you don't need a major-league brain or any credentials. All you need is willingness and courage to try some things—and to accept the fact you're now the proud parent of a man!

Your Son Is a Man

Teen "boys" are young men in all discernible ways. Young and unskilled, for sure, but men in all the ways God intended them to be. I've enjoyed perusing Scripture looking for references to teenagers; the fact is, the Bible never talks about "teenagers." That term is a modern invention. In biblical times, teenagers were referred to as young men. Depending upon which translation you use, Scripture has about one hundred references to "young men."

Any way you cut it, boys become biological men in their early teens. They've got the glands of a man (which generate untold surprises), the body and musculature of a man (which create untold curiosity), the drives, thoughts, desires, and troubles of a man (which combine to produce untold obsessions).

And as early adolescence approaches, a teenager's brain becomes suddenly (over the course of one to three years) more like a man's. He's able to see the world in more abstract ways, just like you. This is perfectly normal, complex brain development. For the first time, he begins to sense hypocrisy, hidden possibility, shades of truth, contradiction, love, and many other things we adults take for granted. The world literally opens up for him in an adultlike way.

So why do you feel like you're losing your son instead of shaping a great, healthy young man? One of the scariest things we parents experience in rearing a teenage son is simply not understanding what's happening inside of him. And as the curtain of life is just rising for him, the curtains are closing on what you're able to see.

Fortunately, teens are not as complicated as they seem. Let me say flatly that it's impossible to predict exactly how an individual teenager will respond to all the radical changes in thinking, hormones, and physical development. But it *is* possible to predict the most important aspect of all: Your son is becoming a man. That means something special in the teen years:

- He will always be in some kind of transition.
- He will try, and succeed, in rebellion against you (count on it).
- He will develop a "secret" life (that has nothing to do with you).
- He likes you and wants you to play a special part in his life.

Let's look briefly at these four areas. Keep one thing firmly in mind as you read: Your son is normal! As you begin to understand your son more, you'll feel less threatened, less defensive, and more capable of guiding him into manhood. In future chapters we'll examine more closely how some of these changes unfold—and how you can use them to your advantage as a parent.

He's Always in Motion

Many cultures celebrate rites of passage when a boy becomes a man. (Actually, in those cultures the rite of passage is not automatic but entails some form of challenge for a boy to prove he is worthy. A kid can't just roll over thirteen on the biological odometer or grow a goatee to join the club.)

In our culture we've eliminated those rituals. For many reasons we try to keep our men boys until they're eighteen (maybe because there are more ways they can get in big trouble than in less "advanced" societies). When most of the population lived on farms or in small communities, people went from being kids directly to being young adults at about the age of thirteen. Now they must wade through this artificial in-between phase we call "adolescence." (Rites-of-passage matters are more fully discussed in chapter 13.)

The collision of nature and biology with culture and social curbing always has behavioral consequences. One of the behavioral consequences arising when young adults traverse adolescence is that they appear to develop through "phases" of increasing maturity. During these phases, young people are experimenting with new ways of acting and thinking, new ways of handling honesty and self-analysis, and so on. These phases complicate our efforts to understand teens and hinder us from giving them what they need. The phases are opaque, as well, hard to predict and manage—but ever present and very powerful.

Let me simplify this: Teenagers are either at transition points in thinking, identity, or social acceptance, or they're coasting quietly somewhere in between. That is all. You can bet that whenever your teen is especially hard to "read" or understand, he is going through a transition time even he doesn't understand.

This transition time may last several weeks to several months. The best thing you can do at that time is to be a mooring for your son, creating a firm anchorage and reference point as he orbits about.

Your Rebel with a Cause

Without a doubt, rebellion—through words, attitudes, or actions—is among parents' top concerns about their teens. In a few short years, the Gerber baby in pajamas turns into James Dean in black leather. He's determined to go his own way, be his own boss, and use any means necessary to give you and your rules the slip!

Here's the rub: Rebellion actually makes a lot of sense. There's a simple reason why your teen balks at your authority: He wants to be free! But there's a catch. You have a legal mandate to control him. To a healthy teen wishing for freedom, you're the person to beat, no matter how nice you are. You're the jailer. It's just human nature for caged people to want freedom.

Your son sees you, his legal guardian, as a tangible threat to his freedom. You're the person to avoid and tolerate when he can't rebel and/or escape. It's the same with the church. And with school. Can you see, for example, how compulsory education—unless properly explained—seems like a barrier rather than a means to success? Teens in full rebellion usually think adults and most institutions exist to strip them of their liberty and their right to be big shots!

So what are we supposed to do? Is there any way to transform this conflict into a win-win?

I think so. First, we have to stop "raising" them. We raise small children. Our teenagers require something entirely different. Now we must learn to *inspire* them, *motivate* them. Somehow we must bridge chasms on their behalf, demonstrating for our teens that we wish to escort them

---

A Closer Focus

For Whom the Curfew Tolls

Weekday and weekend curfews are proven for keeping kids out of harm's way. Your son needs them for his health and peace of mind, and he knows it. Help him learn to work back from the following day's responsibilities.

Try negotiation: Willy wants to stay out Friday till 1:00 A.M. Mom thinks it should be 10:30 P.M. As a compromise, she offers to let him stay out until 11:30 *if* he's able to be in by 11:15 P.M. on three consecutive weekend nights. If he fails, he goes back to 10:30 P.M. and repeats. If he's successful, he's allowed to stay out until 11:30 P.M. for three consecutive weekends. If he's successful, bump it to 12:00 A.M. And so on, civil curfews not withstanding.

Use your judgment, extend trust on trial, and let it be earned thereafter.

toward their dreams, to release them, not to stifle or deprive them.

Later (in chapters 6-8) we'll discuss hot-potato issues surrounding rebellion and learn practical ways to cope that respect a teen's bid for freedom. If we come in peace and wisdom, great things are possible!

The Secret Life of Teenage Boys

I've recently begun to feel distance between me and my own teenagers. I think the feeling is unusually intense because we used to be so close. Now they're pulling away and developing lives that have nothing to do with me. That's left me feeling adrift and alone in the vacuum.

I've tried many different things to draw the kids back toward me, things like asking lots of questions, enticing them with rewards, even the old evil eye that says, *Get over here and talk!* All the standard stuff that worked so well when they were little. Unfortunately, this usually leads to more resistance, which leads to even greater feelings of alienation and desperation in me. Can you relate?

The emotional pain caused by this distance always leads to a skewed view of reality. Suddenly we think our kids are intentionally avoiding us. Every time we see them watching television, for example, we take it as a personal snub. We interpret every vacant glance as an indictment on our value. We see periodic (normal) silence as proof of their hatred.

But hyper-privacy in adolescence is normal. Eventually most kids enter a quiet phase, quietly watching and taking everything in. They don't say much about what's happening inside their heads because frankly they don't understand it much, though they know something's new. And they're desperately trying to figure it all out—for the first time.

This is the beginning of the "secret life" we see in all teenagers. This period is marked by intense privacy and a split between what they show of themselves to you and what they show to others. When your teenage son shuts up, you assume bad things are happening, when in most cases nothing of any vast consequence is occurring.

Don't grind yourself up over your teen's refusal to share everything with you. You did it too. It's part of growing up. As we'll see, this silence doesn't necessarily mean your teen doesn't want to talk or isn't having thoughts! But once you accept that his privacy and silence are part of something not only normal but healthy and positive, you can actually use his silent times for good purpose. We'll find out more about that soon (in chapters 2 and 5).

Every Extreme Case Is an Opportunity

No matter what they say, deep down teenagers really like their parents. That is, they *want* to like them. This news often comes as a great relief to parents left sitting alone in the turbulent backwash of a bad inter-action, wondering where they went wrong. Such reassurance is especially welcome if the wake of the interaction includes such comments as "You're a pain in the rear" or "I wish I didn't have you for parents" or the mother of all hull-smashers, "I HATE you!" Rest assured that your son feels something good about you no matter what he says.

Do you have an "extreme case"? Some teens *are* extreme in their anger, their bitterness, even their hatred—and all the acting out that goes with those feelings. You may be dealing with one (or more) of those situations. I want to acknowledge the painful challenges you may have to face every day. So much ordinary parenting advice doesn't seem to work for you.

Yet in all my years of working with teenagers, I have never met one kid who genuinely wanted to be miserable. Not one. Here is an open-ing—a mustard-seed opportunity—that we'll explore often in this book: Even extreme kids bear a capacity to love and receive love. We all know what can come of something as small as a mustard seed. Your pain and anguish might not disappear with my seemingly small bit of encouragement, but your son has a seed of love that can grow.

Can you see that seed growing today? Maybe not. Maybe you haven't seen the slightest evidence of it for weeks. But the strategic parent has quiet confidence—and a plan.

Parent on a Mission

Over the years one thing has remained constant: teenagers and how they think, act, and live. They've been unfazed by hickory switches, belts, curfews, detention halls, and self-esteem classes. I believe they are one of God's greatest acts of consistency. We cannot possibly change their basic tendencies. What we can change is what we do in response to the predictably alternating sequences of joy and trouble they drag themselves through.

Nobody has all the answers all the time. But as a parent, you can't ever quit searching. I think the words Isser Harrel, former head of the Mossad (Israeli Secret Intelligence), used in describing the qualities of a great secret agent are appropriate for you. Harrel said this agent is "devoted to his homeland, self-sacrificing and resourceful; his prime weapon is his

---

A Closer Focus

The Relationship Comes First

Want respect from your son? Work on your relationship. Want influence, attention? Work on relationship. Relationships take:

- time,
- talk,
- and tolerance.

Parents who hone authentic relationships with their sons are almost always the ones who say raising a teenage boy is great.

intelligence, and his success comes through patience and conscientiousness. If he has gained a world-wide reputation it is because he finds simple and human solutions to his problems."

This is a great mind-set for parents of teenage boys. Forget being Supermom or Superdad. Instead, use your intelligence to find simple, human solutions to human problems. You alone are the expert on your son. In fact, you might consider this book a secret agent's guide to parenting teenage boys. Your mission? To discover who he is without being intrusive. To effect change without losing what matters most to you. To carry on no matter what comes your way.

Because an extraordinary young man is in the making. Right under (or above) your nose.

The Mission of This Book

While it's probably true that past generations of parents didn't share our range of headaches, they had their own troubles with teens. Teenagers have always been willful, emotionally complex and tedious, intense about life, careless, immortal in their own minds, feisty, and idealistic.

But I'm excited about their future too. Every survey I see, every voice I hear, every dream I see leads me to believe that we vastly misunderstand and underestimate this generation of teenagers.

Throughout history, the youth—teens in particular—have always led change. This generation is no different. They're on the lead lap of life. By nature, they want to move and create and change. We must run hard and happily to keep up with them. History shows they won't wait around for us, so let's go! Our future is up for grabs, and we need to find ways to run in their fast lane and help guide them to success.

This *can* be done. It will happen through parents like you who know what they believe and passionately do their jobs well. It's my mission to help you blend those beliefs and passions into patient, deliberate, and methodical parenting. I call it provocative parenting (see chapter 3) because a great parent is one who provokes greatness, who *makes things happen.*

Part of the mission of this book is to help you arrive at some realistic and proven guidelines for shaping your son's inner man—and begin to make it happen. Regardless of what your son does on the outside, you'll sleep better because you'll know his inner man is successfully under construction.

Here's a brief glance at where we're headed:

- You want to change him, and I'm going to help you learn how to provoke change by what you do and say.
- You want to feel connected with your son, but you can't always do this. I'm going to help you learn to communicate better.
- You want to raise him, but instead I'll help you learn to motivate him and inspire him.
- You want him to cooperate, and I'm going to show you how to implement a system that, when necessary, overrides his.
- You want more than anything to matter to your son, to affect his life in a huge way, and starting in the next chapter, I'm going to pepper you with ideas about how to shape and strengthen that invisible inner territory of your son's heart. That's what God made you to want.

You Cannot Fail

As I watch my own sons (Jake, sixteen, and Zac, twelve) develop into men, I keep reminding myself that what I'm watching is young, inexperienced adults making things up as they go along. Life is all new to them. Their actions are, for the most part, entirely predictable, completely human, and simple for a parent like me to prepare for.

What's more, they're very aware of their own weaknesses. What they need is someone willing to believe in them and to see a brighter tomorrow for them. What they need is someone who believes they can change and become the people they secretly long to be.

Most of us have only snapshot memories of teenhood. Too often this isn't enough to recall the pains: feeling as though we didn't fit in, feeling like an outsider, lost and alone, a pathetic loser. If we could recall more of those times, we'd remember how exciting it was to meet an adult who really focused on our strengths. Someone who told us how we'd win rather than how we'd fail.

You can be that person for your teen. That sets you apart in a way worth remembering.

There is no crisis in raising teens other than those you create from your own fears and insecurities. Since you know ahead of time that you'll make errors, relax. You cannot possibly destroy your teenager. They're just too tough, independent, and grown-up. They'll survive and mature, no matter how bad you are. God made them that way.

And as a mom or dad, you're not that bad! You're reading this book, aren't you? You're making an effort, aren't you? You talk to your peers for ideas and insight, don't you? You see? You're already at the front of the class.

You may even want to consider risking some errors on purpose. Why not try some bold new things and see what happens? Why not take a big swing at this parenting-young-men thing and see what you hit?

Chapter Two

Mind over Myth

The truth about your teenager

What's the first thing that comes to mind when I say the words *junior high school teacher, youth worker,* or *teen counselor?* Most people wag their heads and mutter something like, "There ain't enough money to get me to do that," or, "Those poor folks."

But ask those who are successful at handling teenagers, and you'll see and hear a different attitude. Their eyes light up. They'll say their job is the best hard job in the world—and besides, they like the kids.

Teenage boys have a lot of lovable qualities: shiny faces, lots of energy and vigor, belief in invincibility, hubris, humor, and more. They're a Pandora's box. Anything can happen when they're around. And it's *not* always bad. They are wonderful people. I sometimes pity them for having to deal with us!

So what's the problem? For one thing, as a society we believe too many negative stereotypes about teenagers. These cultural labels can easily become self-fulfilling liabilities. Once I spoke to a group of troubled teenagers, and one of the kids in the group, a big kid, was sitting quietly in the corner fidgeting with his fingers. I didn't know what he was doing, nor did I care. But it bugged the principal who presided over our get-together. Midway through my presentation, the principal called me to a halt and verbally ripped this kid for his inattention and his distracting behavior. It was an agonizing moment. I felt especially bad for the kid, because he hadn't been bothering anyone. In response to the public dress-down, this kid "fulfilled the prophecy" about himself and slumped deeper into the corner. Throughout the rest of the presentation, he never did emerge from his emotional cocoon.

After the talk the principal tried to convince me that the boy was a cocaine user and that all the digital fidgeting was chemical. But his friends told me their buddy was just doing what he always does: finger math (an intriguing method of doing calculations with your fingers). But the principal's mythology was set in cement—withdrawn, nervous kids are drug users—and it was making some of his students sink.

Before we get to the truth about your teenager, let's dispel some destructive, or at least pointless, myths. There are probably thousands:

Once in trouble, always in trouble.

The teen years are filled with conflict and strife.

Teenagers are beyond hope.

Teens just don't care.

Teens are dying to take drugs and alcohol.

Teens are a discipline problem.

Teens never talk.

There's a generation gap.

Teens assume all adults are fools.

Teens are obsessed with sex.

Teens look for trouble.

Teens are the puppets of their peers.

Teens are gullible.

Teens are TV addicts.

Teens don't care about success or failure.

Teens never think about God, values, or purpose.

These statements are stereotypes, partial truths that get inflated into "laws." Stereotypes say teenagers are defiant, reckless, and hardheaded. The truth says they are defiant, reckless, and hardheaded *sometimes*. But so, too, are most of the adults we deal with every day. Dealing with teenagers isn't really any different from dealing with any other human being. They have their own unique strengths and weaknesses, biases and values, rules and concerns.

Teenagers are never *always* anything. They are not *always* reckless; they are *sometimes* reckless. Teenagers are not *always* quiet; they are *sometimes* quiet. Teenagers are not *always* flaky; they are *sometimes* flaky (and not as good at hiding it as adults are).

Here's the formula: *My son is not always _____; he is sometimes ____.* Think about your son. Take a moment to fill in the formula with one or two specific problems your kid gives you.

Most teenagers make great decisions. Most stay away from drugs, avoid car wrecks, do acceptable schoolwork, and so on. I'm not going to say teenagers are always great decision makers. They make some really stupid mistakes and very bad judgments from time to time. We read in the papers every day stories about teenagers losing their lives due to a single bad choice. It's a reality.

However, we must be fair. Our kids make many good decisions that we don't often notice or credit them for. If we do nothing more than grant them the respect they deserve for the good choices they make, we will do them a great service. And if we can free ourselves from the tyranny of partial truths, we can begin to parent successfully with the whole truth in mind.

In the first chapter I reminded you that your son is a man in most respects. Before we start working on parenting tactics, we need to look more closely at who your young man really is. I'm going to share a few things that generally hold true about how teenage boys think and behave. These statements are not intended to stereotype teenage men but, just the opposite, to educate you and open your mind to behaviors boys consistently express.

The Truth in Three Parts

Trying to understand and assimilate all that's been written about how young men think and grow emotionally is like trying to hold fog. Just about the time you think you've got it—*poof!*—it's gone. What motivates your teen? How does he make decisions? Is he really thinking anything important? These are important questions that deserve clear answers.

The understanding of human psychological development is a fine blend of good science, bright insight and observation, old wives' tales, and rumors. Trying to separate what you actually need to know from all the misinformation is tricky. But you need only a few very simple principles to understand your teenage boy. To make this easy, let's talk about the three elements of growth that probably concern you most: Your teen's heart (his emotions), his mind (his thinking), and his soul (his spiritual core).

Pleasure and Pain: The Heart of a Teen

As adults, our thinking and decision making are based on a wide range of facts, insights, concepts, predictions, and hunches. And, oh yes, emotions. Teenage boys make decisions on a far simpler level. All they really care about is pleasure and pain. On a practical level, this simple distinction is all you need to know about their emotional life to understand and predict how they'll act.

Let's step backward and take a broader look at emotions. Almost every emotion you and I feel is built upon different combinations of pleasure and pain. Nothing else. We discuss emotions like they're distinct and real, but they're not—at least, not like a rock or a sunset is real. Boys are even more fundamental. For instance, teenage boys don't get "depressed"; they just feel a certain level of internal pain that we label "depression." The label is only, well, a label. Too often we trip over these vague labels that really tell us very little about what someone is feeling. Labels are really just a verbal indexing system that people use to try to relate with each other.

This distinction is crucial, because teens think and make decisions, not on the basis of the more complex, emotional blends of adults, but on vastly more simple experiences: He feels good; he feels bad. If you want to understand how your son thinks and decides, begin thinking in terms of pleasure and pain exclusively.

Here's an 80/20 rule you can use to understand how pleasure and pain affect your son: 80 percent of his behaviors are explained by 20 percent of the possible pleasure/pain combinations. Five pleasure/pain combinations dominate young men. Memorize these five combinations, and you'll understand what controls 80 percent of your son's actions.

1. Pain in the present
2. Pain in the future
3. Pleasure in the present
4. Pleasure in the future
5. Curiosity now

Let me briefly explain these. Pain in the present is any internal discomfort he feels now. This can include sadness, anxiety, worry—you know the menu. You can expect him to try wild means to escape present pain. Not many young guys will wallow in a pool of misery for long. They hate it.

Pain in the future is similar. As you'll see soon, teenage men have an emerging ability to forecast life. You can count on your son to act in ways to avoid pools of pain.

What he seeks is pleasure in the present. He doesn't care too much what the pleasure is. He just wants to feel comfort and ease. Emotionally, he's like a cow: All he wants to do is graze in the grass and feel good all day.

But teenagers are learning to forecast their pleasures and plan on them. Pleasure in the future becomes a great motivator, especially as your son gets older.

And finally, there's curiosity. In my opinion, this is the single most powerful urge teenage boys—and the rest of us, for that matter—can feel. It is a gift that powers a large swath of behavior. We hunger to discover things, and we're driven to satisfy this odd hunger. Like pain and pleasure, it's a simple, human thing. Your teen son is curious and will consistently act upon his curiosities.

How can we use this simple pleasure/pain principle to parent teenagers?

First, understand that teenage boys make decisions from their own world-view. They choose what they do because they're making what seems *to them* to be wise, sensible choices (even though they're often not). A young man can be counted on to make decisions that he believes will benefit himself—to increase pleasure and decrease pain.

Second, young men are groping around in life like it's a dark room. It reminds me of an icebreaker I sometimes use when I'm speaking to groups. People are assigned to one of four groups—horses, cows, goats, or pigs—then we turn out the lights and they have to find each other and assemble into groups by animal sounds alone. In the same way, teenagers spend a lot of time stumbling around, latching on to anything that looks friendly or familiar. Nowhere is this more noticeable than in their decision making. Why? They're drawn toward pleasures and curiosities and away from pain.

Part of a parent's continuing challenge is to turn on the light to show the teen what's *really* motivating him. What he may describe in terms of logic is often nothing more than pure desire. But if we can understand

---

A Closer Focus

Screening Behavior

Karl Marx, founder of communism, said religion was the opiate of the people. But he never had chat rooms. Or Doom. Or Netscape Navigator.

Computers are going to dominate your son's future. He must learn to use them. A parent's challenge is to bring balance, context, and good moral choices to this activity as with any potential obsession. I'd almost always rather have my sons in front of a computer than in front of a television. But two hours a day is enough.

Many of the sports, educational, and skill-building games young men can play on computers are extremely violent and dark. In addition, just being online opens up your home to a deluge of potentially offensive material. In our home we apply the same rules to computer games and online material that we do music or printed material (see chapter 10). We make it a point to talk about situations that violate our family's values.

Use parental online guards as needed, but remember your son is probably smart enough to get around them if he really wants to. Consider keeping the setup where your son can be part of the family—and you can be "hawk-eyed." A clear discussion of expectations and consequences is your best ally.

You own the computer, or at least the electrical supply that runs it.

---

what's driving him, we'll have a much better idea how to utilize these forces for good while nudging him toward maturity.

The Great Brain Robbery: The Mind of a Teen

To clarify how young men think, let's briefly review how preteen kids think. In general, kids prior to the age of seven are immersed in a concrete world. To understand what's going on around them, they must touch, feel, poke, sniff, prod, bang, fiddle, and taste. Life is what they can gather through their senses. Show a bunch of five-year-olds a pail of worms, and before long someone will try eating one! They have a very limited ability to think abstractly, so they seek experience. Their world has no grays. They think in black/white, right/wrong, good/bad. Life is simple.

Somewhere between the ages of seven to ten, a major leap in brain complexity kicks in. This changes everything. Practically overnight kids start thinking like adults, in that they:

- develop abstract concepts
- reason abstractly
- utilize reliable logic
- develop self-consciousness
- see "gray areas" of life
- develop perspective
- understand two sides of a story
- grasp cause and effect
- develop interpersonal perceptions
- apply reverse logic
- read hypocrisy and lies in others
- create self-expectations
- discover cynicism, sarcasm, and more

In a flash, your baby becomes a brand-spanking-new adult! And it was all biologically driven. You had nothing to do with it.

One of the first results of this swift brain development is the onset of a quiet period. As soon as a young boy gains a sense of self-consciousness—"I'm here, this is me, and I'm not like you at all"—he will instinctively withdraw and watch for a while. We fast-paced adults may not even notice it in our teens, but this quiet period can take weeks, months, or years to grow through. It's perfectly normal.

A second result of this rise in thinking ability is the development of a personal life that has nothing to do with you. Suddenly your boy will comprehend the power of withholding information. He will discover that he can do all kinds of things without your knowledge—or consent. He will also find out the world can be an unforgiving place. Pleasure and pain take on a whole new meaning to him.

A Closer Focus

The Heart of the Matter

Often a parent doesn't know where to start with a teenager because problems swirl together into an overwhelming mess. To get in control, try separating and identifying what the key issues really are. Make a list of the things bothering you about your teenager. Then narrow the list by determining what all those things have in common. For example, say the problems are occasional lying, silence, and withdrawal. Do they have one thing in common? In this case, it may be lack of personal, private "down time" or bad attitudes or unresolved arguments that need to be talked through. Choose one and act on it. As you reduce your problem list, you'll be surprised to discover that usually just a few simple things really need attention.

Remember that he is experiencing all these things for the very first time. His quietness does not suggest he's devised a grand scheme to lie or keep things hidden from you. He doesn't hate you, no matter what you find out he's been holding back. He's not "turning bad," no matter how much he keeps you in the dark. It's just that all these new experiences are a complete novelty to his new brain.

Remember, too, he's only vaguely aware he's going through all this! Suddenly he's seeing the world for the very first time through completely new eyes—and suspects that he's the first and only one to see all this complexity. He feels like a pioneer, the first to discover a brave new world. This can lead to arrogance and self-confidence, and he can begin to say things that make parents roll their eyes. Gems like, "Who are *you* to tell *me* about the realities of life!"

We all need to be patient. We can outlast this phase.

This developing awareness and reasoning ability are also combined with an array of other thinking gifts. Intelligence is no less than a combination of seven of them. Every person has all seven intelligences but in unique, individual combinations. (Howard Gardner, a well-respected Harvard psychologist, has successfully debunked the idea that intelligence is a single-dimension IQ score.)

The seven dimensions of intelligence are:

1. Artistic intelligence (skilled in the visual arts)
2. Logic-mathematical intelligence
3. Spatial intelligence (gifted in spatial relationships)
4. Musical intelligence
5. Physical intelligence (athletic and physically adept)
6. Interpersonal intelligence (good at dealing with others)
7. Intrapersonal intelligence (a good understanding of self)

Every young man is great at some of these and not so good at others.

Let's get more specific: Every young man is *becoming*, or *has the potential to become*, great at a unique combinations of these gifts.

Your young man is gifted in several areas that perhaps you haven't thought of before. Wise parents observe what their son excels at, then feed that gift like a roaring fire. Wise parents continually look for opportunities to stretch their young guy in ways that encourage his strong points.

I hope you're beginning to sense that an exciting panorama is opening up before you if you'll...

- put down lazy, hurtful myths about your son;
- keep a clearheaded grasp of how pain, pleasure, and curiosity motivate him; and
- accept (and rejoice) in your son's exciting new adventures in thinking, feeling, and experiencing the world.

Suddenly a vibrantly successful and genuinely enjoyable parent-and-son journey can become a reality at your house.

And we haven't even added the most amazing dimension of all.

Soul Man: The Soul of a Teen

In today's society, it's often unorthodox to discuss the soul of a teen. It seems unscientific, thus lacking serious merit. Yet it's high time we consider unorthodox things in our quest to raise great men.

When I talk about the soul, I start with my belief that everyone has a deep core, something about them that is true, consistent, and unchanging. That core can be quite good, or it can be quite bad. We all have a core of beliefs and attitudes that make up what we really think. Some of those beliefs and attitudes are worthy of pride, others of contempt. That's why we're so careful about sharing that stuff with others.

The awareness of that inner core begins in the early teenage years.

The wrestling match with that core, the real inner self, begins then too. That is why, when we talk about a teenager's core, his soul, we're really talking about ourselves too.

Jesus spoke extensively about these deep recesses. To better understand how to help our sons grow their souls, we should better understand what Jesus thought about our souls. He made no age-related distinctions on this matter. What He did say was that everyone needs to come clean about what's deep inside of him or her. He deeply admired lack of guile and simple honesty.

That's a good place to start, especially in this personal identity-obsessed time in which we live. For a teenager, getting an identity is like trying on new clothes. He looks and searches until he finds something he likes, then he wears it for a while to see if he likes the look and feel. If he does, he keeps it. If he doesn't, he goes searching for something that makes him feel better.

It's all window dressing on the soul.

Deep inside each young man is a growing awareness of goodness and badness. Along with this is a growing sense of personal limits and the need for faith. Despite his extensive self-promotion, omnipotence, and hubris, deep down inside he has a growing sense of who he is, for better or worse.

Most teenagers don't like what they see. That's normal, and in the right atmosphere, it's all right.

What's the right atmosphere for your son? You want to help him see that his soul, good or bad, is the one God created him with and that he can do something with it. You can help create that kind of atmosphere by providing him options worthy of exploration. You cannot stop your son from looking for new identities to dress up his deeply felt soul. What you want to do is provide good identities for him to try on. Don't shove down his throat what you believe him to be, but act as more of a tour guide, showing him the options. Be a coach and a mentor. This requires patience and faith on your part and an open mind on his.

Teens Are It!

I'll confess that I used to have bad attitudes toward teenagers. I had these bad attitudes because I was too lazy to get to know any teenagers and because I was intimidated by them. They felt foreign to me, and I never thought they would accept me because I was an alien (read that, *adult*).

One day I decided to do an experiment. I would change my attitude. I decided to like teenagers. I began talking to them in public places, confidently approaching them when I saw them, interacting with them at schools. I'd sit and talk with kids, kids I knew and kids I didn't know, whenever I could.

Okay, I made some funny blunders. At times I looked like a fool. And often I was scared. But I quickly learned this truth: *Teens are more frightened of me than I am of them!* And I discovered that not only does friendliness work, but it's really fun!

Try my experiment. Seek out teenage boys and befriend them. Your devotion to and appreciation of them will skyrocket.

Now that you know you are raising a man and you understand more about how he thinks and operates, you're ready to learn some strategies.

Chapter Three

Meet the Provocative Parent

Six principles that put you in charge

The Reverend Eugene F. Rivers III of Azusa Christian Church in Boston has never forgotten the advice he once got from a drug kingpin.

Rivers wanted to spearhead an effort to clean up his community. He wanted to focus on helping kids whose lives were being ruined by drug addiction, gang violence, and joblessness. In a stroke of genius, he decided to ask the local drug dealers for insight. With their fancy clothes and Cadillacs, they seemed to be the real heroes to kids.

"Man, why did we lose you to the underworld?" he asked one powerful deal maker. "And why are we losing other kids to you right now?"

The answer was stunning. The dealer stared him in the eye and said, "I'm there—you're not! When the kids go to school, I'm there—you're not. When the boy goes for a loaf of bread or wants a pair of sneakers or just somebody older to talk to or feel safe and strong around, I'm there—you're not. I'm there—you're not. I win. You lose."

I don't want to lose with my kids, and I know you don't either. We want to win. Moms and dads, crazy as it sounds, it's time we take the advice of a drug dealer.

It's time to show up in a big way.

I don't mean just hang out or be available or run the carpool, but show up in such a way that our presence and influence are strong, visible, and effective. Adults—whether drug lords or successful parents—who are most successful with kids are present in powerful, colorful, and in-your-face ways. They don't accomplish their goals by simply hoping teens will follow their good example. They have a plan:

- They provide clear and positive acceptance.
- They encourage and reinforce honest communication.
- They let teens know they're liked and that they "belong."
- They're enthusiastic—no stick-in-the-muds allowed.
- And they show up to make it happen.

Too often we parents drop the ball because we think "showing up" is the same thing as mumbling about homework from behind a newspaper or delivering couch potato speech 19 with slightly more starch than 18.

Unless you have a plan and make it work, someone else's system will run your teen's life. The more I work with teens and their parents, the more I see moms and dads abdicating their power and influence to somebody else. Some have simply given up, believing they can't compete against their son's world of attractive influences. This strikes me as short-sighted and irresponsible.

What happens as a result of this surrender and meandering? We float along, praying for miracles. In short, we relinquish the chance to even have a system and end up with no plans, no approach, and no steps for getting where we want to go with our kids. Another system is in charge—television, movies, music, influential peers, the wrong crowd. Their world is full of kingpins with enormous influence.

What I suggest is an "in-your-face," audacious approach I call *provocative parenting*. The idea is to be a cause, not an effect; to be an active, unapologetic variable rather than a passive nonvariable; to make family life fun and interesting; to set high goals and reach them with your son.

The Master of Surprise

Jesus was the ultimate example of provocative leadership. He didn't influence His "children" by sitting back and hoping that people would like Him and agree with Him. He loved to startle, to use contradictions, to stride into "no trespassing" zones.

To apply this approach to parenting requires artistry and stealth. After all, parenting teens is done in an atmosphere of intense suspicion, friction, and occasional rivalry. Not exactly the kind of atmosphere that conjures up Norman Rockwell images.

Where do you begin? Think about this: Teenage men live in a provocative world. You can hear it in their music, their relationships, their cars, and their competitive sports. Their hopes and affections thrive on energy and excitement. The very nature of teenage boys calls for a parenting approach that respects and complements that zest.

Don't get nervous. Provocative parenting is not so much about who you are but about what you do. It relies on a set of principles that any parent can learn and apply. It doesn't rely on personality, age, or interests. Any parent who cares about his or her teenage son can be a provocative, high-impact parent.

Here's one of the major differences between the local drug dealer and you. He wants influence for a bad end. You want influence for your son's best—and you're willing to take a major leap of faith to provoke it into reality. Trust me. If a despicable gangland drug runner can win the allegiance of a teenager, so can you.

Six Principles of Provocative Parenting

Throughout this book, we will apply six principles of provocative parenting to problem areas we most worry about: communication, sexuality, discipline, rites of passage, leadership development, and spiritual life. The six principles will provide an invisible backdrop as we tackle each of these areas.

We've already encountered the first rule of a provocative parent. Let me restate principle 1: Don't just be there; be audaciously present.

Now we're ready to look one by one at the other five principles of provocative parenting:

- Don't try to force change; provoke it.
- Don't just have a good attitude; get a great metaphor.
- Don't tolerate teens; get passionate about them.
- Don't get a bigger hammer; get a better idea.
- Have fun.

Before we go any further, I want to dispel the possible misunderstanding that provocative parenting means being easy, fun-loving, or permissive.

How many times have we heard a dad say, "I'm my son's best buddy," because he coaches the peewee football team. Or, "If I'm his friend and I believe the best about him, he'll do just fine." Or how about, "I don't want to make him rebel by having rules. So I focus on having fun with him and being his pal"?

Parents like this mistakenly believe they're having an impact on their sons. In reality their parenting is passive and flaccid. Teens already have buddies. What they need is a strong parent first who can be a great friend second.

Write this in big letters in your head: *To be provocative is to make things happen in and concerning my son, to be a visible and felt influence on him, to powerfully affect him for a lifetime of good.*

Principle 2: Don't Try to Force Change—Provoke It

A lot of people hate change. The reason they cringe at change is because it usually happens to them against their will. These folks rarely initiate change but merely endure it and feel victimized in the process.

Parents who successfully manage change adopt a different perspective. They instigate change because they enjoy it and have learned how to make the most of it. For provocative parents, this means resolving to get ahead of the curve—to make change work for them, not against them.

This isn't that hard to do. It's possible to embrace change and love it. You can learn how to create change. To do this you must first understand one simple truth: Change yourself and the whole world must adapt. The world, and all those in it, will follow your lead every time. Causes beget effects, especially with boys.

Try this experiment. Get two pennies and lay them flat on a table. Take one of the pennies and slide it up against the second. Now try to push the second penny in a straight line across the table. It's not easy. You'll find the second penny sliding off to the right or left even though you don't seem to be doing anything to make it turn!

The truth is, you are subtly affecting the direction of the penny you push. Though you don't feel it, the swerving path of the pushed penny proves you're doing something different with it than you expect. But with a little practice you can make the pushed penny move straight by adjusting the first penny very subtly right to left as you scoot it. You can learn to do this.

Now increase the challenge. Try adding a third penny and moving it and the second penny in a straight line. It's very hard. You must think through how each movement of the penny you control affects not

The Trouble with Friends

Trying to impose your will on your son's choice of friends is almost always misinterpreted and can backfire badly. Treat your son's peers with respect, dignity, and kindness, no matter how you really feel about them.

But nobody expects you just to have no opinion or do nothing if you see trouble. The reason most conversations about peers blow up is because the timing is wrong. Keep your thoughts to yourself until your son is open and relaxed.

Peer relationships are always in a state of flux. Today they might be best buds and tomorrow hardly have anything nice to say about each other, then the next they're back to best pals again, all's forgiven. Be careful not to get on the wrong side of a cycle.

Remember that your son wants relationships with both you and his peers—he'd rather not have to choose sides. Try not to polarize this situation by making absent-minded, negative comments or cutting remarks. In the long run, you will be among your son's best, most trusted friends. Offer the quality of friendship that demonstrates what he should be looking for in others.

only the second penny but the third too! With some practice, you can control the first penny so well that you can make both pennies travel in a straight line.

The Provocative Penny

In many ways, human relationships work according to an identical law. If you choose, you can be the provoker (the first penny) and make other pennies (including your teenage son) adapt to you. With a little practice and patience, you can get people in your life to react in all kinds of ways. I'm not talking about using them for our own ends or practicing uncaring manipulation. To be a wise and strategic "cause" in your family is one of the most mature kinds of parental love.

This is provocative parenting principle 2: Don't try to force change—provoke it.

The laws operating in the pushed penny are actually profound and analogous to those of highly effective parents. Small changes you make as a parent create large movements in your son. Critical turns in your path affect him whether or not he permits it. You're a change agent capable of forcing action in any direction you like. You can push the penny—your son—to the left or the right depending on what you do. Somebody's gotta decide—it might as well be you.

Still wondering how? You become a change master by watching. Subtly change your behavior and notice what happens. For example, rather than yelling orders across the room, snuggle up close to him and whisper in his ear (mouthwash recommended) and watch what he does. Rather than scold him, ask questions about his future and watch what he does. Rather than criticize his pals, offer to take them out to eat and watch what he does. Get the idea? Will he react like he's always reacted? No. He can't. He's a penny in a row.

A parent interested in exceptional results will always be asking, "Who's the cause and who's the effect in this relationship right now? Who's the master of change at my table? Who's pushing the pennies around here anyway?" As the parent in the house, the advantage is yours to be the instigator of positive action. This won't always make you the most popular person, but it will put you in a much better position to change a life.

Principle 3: Don't Just Get an Attitude; Get an Awesome Metaphor

Your beliefs control how you act, even if you don't know what those beliefs are. Most parents believe much more about their parenting than they realize. Many of their beliefs are "underground," in a sense, unseen but in total control of events. Beliefs control you by limiting the options you think you have. If you want more flexibility as a parent, you must identify those hidden beliefs to be certain they're not secretly subverting you.

How do you unmask your hidden beliefs? Simple. Utilize something Jesus did often. Jesus' daily mission was to reveal the kingdom of heaven to everyone He met. This wasn't easy considering the mind-blowing potential of the truths He taught.

So Jesus spun many illustrations, likening what was unknown about the kingdom of heaven to what was known to His listeners. He called His stories parables. We call them similes or metaphors, figures of speech that compare one thing to another. In Matthew 13, Jesus said the kingdom is like:

- "a man who sowed good seed in his field" (v. 24)
- "treasure hidden in a field" (v. 44)
- "a merchant looking for fine pearls" (v. 45)

The word picture we carry in our heads about an activity has enormous power to shape what we experience. I was once asked to talk to a singles group called "Only the Lonely." The group was really a drag, but not because the people wanted to be that way. None of them wanted to be outcasts. But "Only the Lonely" had become a devastating identity they acted out.

It was so depressing. These folks were bitter and resentful. A few even chided me for being so effervescent when, as one woman said, "Life is harsh." This collective belief that "life is harsh, and we're lonely" had twisted their experience. They had completely lost sight of a bigger truth—the opportunity, adventure, and friendship that a group like theirs could offer.

To become a provocative and highly effective parent of a teenage boy, the word pictures you use to describe your teen have to work *for* you, not against you. If your metaphors are filled with negativity,

A Closer Focus

Metaphorically Speaking

Write down a word picture describing something your son does well and something he does very poorly. Then, for fun, see if you can use the metaphor for the thing he does well as a replacement for the thing he does poorly. For example, "he's a tiger on the soccer field" (he's aggressive and smart) and "he's a slug in math class" (he's lazy and unresponsive). Play around with these metaphors as though they were toys. Notice the swirl of feelings you create inside yourself. Think through how you might treat your "tiger in math class" differently—and help provoke change—if you made a radical change in word pictures.

aversion, difficulty, and hopelessness, you must alter them before anything else will change.

Word Pictures with Impact

Ask yourself, "What's the big picture here? Is my mental picture about my teenager part of the problem or part of the solution?" Using a word picture, how would you describe parenting your teen? Following Jesus' lead, try filling in this sentence:

"Parenting my teenage boy is like _____."

You might come up with all sorts of images and thoughts. You might even have several, depending on different circumstances. Do any of your similes sound like these? Parenting my teen is like:

- herding a rabbit (I don't get anywhere chasing him—but whip out the carrots, and he comes running.)
- building sand castles (Just about the time I think we've made a connection, those waves roll in.)
- baking bread (If I just take my time and pay attention to the details, he'll turn out fine.)
- pulling teeth (I have to yank all day just to get this guy to speak!)

Your word pictures for parenting your boy reflect the truth about how you perceive the relationship. In other words, your pictures are probably attached to real feelings and experiences. Your word pictures also suggest how you probably act in his presence.

Metaphors have limits. Notice how many parables Jesus used to teach new things about one subject. A bunch! Choosing a more positive word picture won't cure all your parenting problems, by any means, but it's a great place to start. Especially if you want to become a parent who makes good things happen.

Principle 4: Don't Get a Bigger Hammer;
Get a Better Idea

Fearlessly and constantly ask yourself this simple question: "Is what I'm doing to influence this young man working?"

Be radically honest. We get hooked into cycles of thoughtless parenting, blindly believing that we're doing our best. It's difficult to admit we're wrong or need to change when we cling to "But I'm doing my best!" There's no room for improvement if we've sold ourselves on that baloney.

Let me illustrate this another way. Figuratively speaking, some people solve every problem they encounter by smacking it with a hammer. If a problem becomes unfixable, rather than admit failure, they reach for a bigger hammer. They assume that applying just a little more of what didn't work in the first place is the answer.

Not true—at least most of the time.

Take arguing, for example. A man who wanted to win debates with his son once asked me for help. I confessed that I'm not a great debater, and being curious about his motives, I asked why he would want to do that anyway. He explained that his son was being bad (he was doing normal teenager stuff), and the dad was failing in his attempts to explain the boy's evil treacheries to him (he wasn't winning the debate). He told me he'd listened to tapes on debating, written out scripts, practiced in front of a mirror, even consulted a theater director.

This dad didn't take into account what was happening inside his son's head. Young men make decisions for their own reasons, and they're not always logical. In fact, the young guy probably wasn't thinking about logic at all. Instead he probably wondered why his dad loved pummeling him with his stupid ideas! The only message getting through to the kid from Dad was, "I don't care about you as much as I care about proving that I'm smarter and stronger."

Parents stuck in bigger-hammer thinking believe they just need a more powerful version of whatever isn't working, whether the hammer is talking, bribing, debating, or punishing.

Provocative parents choose to do something different. If a "hammer" fails to work, they quickly move to screwdrivers. If a screwdriver fails, they try a velvet glove. If that fails, they try butterfly kisses. They're always trying new things. Flexibility and experimentation are the keys. These parents end up relaxed and at ease because their style is not to make their solution work but to find what works through open-minded exploration

A Closer Focus

Money Smarts

Teenage boys love money. I've always encouraged my boys that they can have as much as they want. Help yourself. We live in America, and you can have all you like. That's when they discover that it doesn't fall out of the sky like snow. They have to work for it.

I pay for spot labor rendered by my kids and allow them to make promises of future effort if I give them substantial amounts of money ahead of time. This system has allowed our kids to learn the value of work and reward. I always pay them immediately. If they borrow money, they must work it off immediately. I frequently give tips, and I charge interest on borrowed funds (and pay interest if I'm the borrower). It becomes a very lifelike economy.

Help your son not only save money but get started in rudimentary investing. Perhaps you could enroll your son in an investing club or have him talk to a banker or financial planner about investment opportunities open to a young man. Online brokerages offer additional real-life training opportunities.

of alternative solutions. They aren't afraid to admit that what they're doing is a total wash and it's time to move on. Maybe to kicking butt. Maybe to hysterical laughter at themselves.

After all, there's a lot of riding room out there on the range of better ideas.

Shed Some Skin

Let me illustrate how admitting you're wrong can open doors to success. A very prim, soft-spoken woman approached me several months after I'd spoken to her church about handling teenagers. During that talk I'd told them about the principle "if what you're doing is not working, do something else." Now she was anxious to share with me the radical results she'd had with her boy the evening after my talk.

He'd been troubling her on several issues. Her normal approach to handling him boiled down to pleading for cooperation. Pleading seemed the only thing left to do. But his spiraling antagonism proved to her that he had no real interest in making the situation better. So she made a brave decision to shed the old skin and try on a whole new personality.

That night she needed to confront her son about staying out too late the previous evening. She decided to use gut-level honesty. No whining, no conditions, no requests—just some shocking new information. Careful to avoid pleas, she sat down and started revealing to him that she herself had been a troublemaker as a teenager. She hadn't cared about what her parents thought. The surprised son asked uncomfortable questions, and she gave uncomfortably candid replies. Then she went on to tell her son—adult to adult—about how painful the long-term consequences of that lifestyle had been for her and her family.

For the first time in a long time, her teenage boy listened to every word. He had mistakenly believed his mom was a weak-willed, lily-white

saint. How could she understand his world? But his close encounter with "the real mom" changed everything. "For the first time," she told me, "we had a heart-to-heart talk. I could tell that I had really touched him inside."

That evening they agreed that he would notify her of his where-abouts, and she in turn would not badger him. In her words, "It worked!" Just by putting down the old hammer. Shedding the old skin.

It's not easy shelving your ego, your comfortable routines, even your comfortable correctness. But if you're willing to candidly question how you do things, then be prepared to change what you're doing if it's going nowhere. You will provoke an incredible response in your son. And you may never reach for that hammer again.

Principle 5: Don't Just Tolerate Teens; Get Passionate About Them

In the last chapter, I briefly described my experience with learning to like teenagers. Let me describe another attitude I've seen often among people who have great relationships with teenage boys.

As I said, I used to feel a lot of panic when I spent time with teenagers socially, though I counseled and coached them privately with great success. Every time I was with a group of teens, I felt like I was in a cage with lions that would just as soon eat me as talk to me. They intimidated me, made me feel on edge. I believed they were highly judgmental and would reject me based on my age alone.

You could say my metaphor—"teens are nasty lions"—was not working for me.

It all changed when I made the decision to change my point of view. I changed it to: "These crazy creatures aren't man-eating lions! They're a bunch of frightened kids, more scared than I am. They want someone

to walk up to them, talk to them, like them—maybe even tickle them under the chin."

I immediately started to wade into crowds of teens whenever possible. I treated them like a bunch of quivering little kitties in need of a gentle scratch. They loved it. Soon I did too. In fact, by stretching myself and mixing with these kids I bumped into other truly gifted adults who also enjoyed their times with these young people. As we talked, these gifted adults shared with me their mind-sets, allowing me to feel even more at home and confident with teenagers I met. Now the tension I used to feel in a teenager's presence is long gone.

When you begin to like teenagers *on purpose*, something powerful happens. Think about the strongest, most positive, visceral feeling you have for your son. A special message of love and strength is transmitted when you focus on that feeling. Your son is waiting to sense that message from you. Act on the best things you feel toward your son.

Principle 6: Have Some Fun!

Above all the passions you provoke, I pray that having fun is at the top of the list. There's nothing worse in the realm of parenting than a joyless crank. Generations of well-intentioned, perfectly correct, biblically informed parents have gone down to defeat because their kids figured out something vital—the joy was missing. Laughs never happened. Fun had to be bought somewhere else.

Adults can overlook somberness in the duty of doing good, but teenagers never can. For them, humor and rejoicing are the proof of any pudding. Let me tell you that family fun has a way of salving the deepest wounds we encounter as we nurture our sons through adolescence.

I learned this lesson from a happy mother of several successful teenagers. She is fifty, but her vim makes her look mid-thirtyish. In jest, I once asked her if she ever had any problems in her life.

"Well, I never really stopped to think about it," she said. "It's just life, and I'm trying to make the best of it."

A smile slowly creased her face as she finished. "Bill, finding fun, looking for it, has saved my sanity many times. I look for fun so much that it's just become natural. There really are so many things to smile about."

The world of teenagers is a dynamic and unpredictable place. No single idea, philosophy, piece of wisdom, or input hits all of them the same way every time. Successful parenting "techniques" won't succeed all the time. And teenage boys exhibit a breathtaking array of responses to everything. That's why I highly recommend that you determine to celebrate your teen at every opportunity. And that you develop a stubborn readiness to laugh at life.

Tightly grip your sense of humor. Please understand that a sense of humor has nothing to do with your ability to deliver a one-liner, be the life of the party, or be the grooviest parent on the block. Nothing.

But if you find ways to laugh at even the intractable and mind-boggling problems you encounter as a parent of a teenage boy, you will be dispensing God's most amazing grace. He honors those who achieve enough humility, peace, and surety about things to smile (the Bible calls it faith, hope, and love).

Let fun be part of your purposeful parenting plan, and your son will see the spark of our Savior in you. It may be your most provocative move yet.

Chapter Four

Impossibility Parenting

Restacking the odds for parents in extreme circumstances

I've spoken to many "impossibility parents"—single parents, foster parents, dads working the night shift, spouses of substance abusers, wives of workaholics, families in prolonged financial chaos, parents of handicapped children.... If you're one, you surely know it.

Some of you are happy. A few of you feel your dreams are coming true. Most of you feel like failures a lot of the time. All of you feel a great deal of isolation and sadness. And all of you are tired and stressed to the max. Let's see if we can find a way through the morass.

God intended kids to be raised in normal two-parent units. Nobody would argue against that. But take heart: A great marriage and a lack of significant problems don't guarantee that a family will raise great kids. Likewise, families that face chronic and serious challenges don't necessarily lead kids to failure. Every family, every life, must face different combinations of challenges and resources.

What each mom and dad must do is find out how to be successful despite the obstacles—to find the possibilities hiding in the daily onslaught.

You see it's only right that I tell you that I don't believe in the word *impossible*. Parenting is hard, yes. Ridiculous, definitely. Overwhelming at times, sure. But impossible—not really. As much as anything, it's parents like you who have convinced me that amazing things are possible when we bring our whole wills and God's whole, powerful goodness to bear on a seemingly intractable parenting problem.

Teenage Boys! is not specifically written for parents who are in "impossible" circumstances. But nearly all of what is presented here can help. Even when life all by itself is provocative enough, thank you very much, there's truth and help to be found in everyday wisdom. That is my hope and prayer for you. Allow me to show you what I mean.

More Than Twice the Load

Several years ago, my wife, Kathi, and I were asked to write a series of articles for Focus on the Family's *Single Parent* magazine. Preparing to write those articles, we did several things. First, we asked several single parents we knew to complete a questionnaire on their single-parenting needs and challenges. Next, we did extensive phone interviews to clarify their input and comments. Finally, I did what, for me, was the closest I could get to being a single dad: I asked Kathi to quit taking care of the house for a week and let me do everything.

The second most memorable outcome of the week was that Kathi wanted me to extend the research. Kathi works, so I understood her glee. But what stood out most to me during that week was this—total, relentless exhaustion. The exhaustion affected my outlook, the way I interacted with the kids, and my consistency. I could've been lean and in shape, eaten energy bars, drunk coffee, and had Surge for dessert, and they still wouldn't have revived me.

If you're a single or otherwise overburdened parent, your load is more than twice that of "normal" parents. Perhaps someone in your home is physically handicapped, neglectful, or gone. Your job is the challenge of a lifetime.

I'm writing this chapter to help lighten your load. I know you may not accept some of the suggestions I'm going to make. Maybe you've tried them already. Maybe you haven't got time. But I want you to know that when I make suggestions I feel sensitive to your heavy load, and I respect what little energy you have available.

Yet there's nothing about shaping your boy into a fine young man that is beyond your reach. You may have to redefine success. You *will* have to go easy on yourself. But you can still raise an extraordinary young man no matter what your situation is. You have "the power of one"— and with the right approach you can multiply that power tremendously. Many people have.

If some of the ideas I share with you sound like old news, rather than discard them, I encourage you to revisit each one. Great ideas often take many attempts to work out right. Resist the temptation to say, "I've tried that already, and it didn't work." Try again. Make a heroic effort. Just maybe something will be different this time.

Something *will* be different this time.

On any day, you're just that close to being a *possibility* parent.

Several obstacles litter the path to success for parents in your circumstances. Here are three power-of-one rules that apply especially to single parents. Others of you may also find useful parallels:

1. Get some depth perspective.
2. Negotiate with your saboteurs.
3. Consult the opposite gender.

Power-of-One Rule 1: Get Some Depth Perspective

If you're single or generally alone in your parenting, your life is two-dimensional—one dimension too few. Let me explain.

Binocular vision (the ability to perceive depth) is the result of having two eyes looking at the same object at the same time. Parenting alone is like having an eye poked out. Your depth perception regarding people is very restricted. Kathi and I have been married almost nineteen years. In that time I cannot tell you how often I've looked at a situation with one of our kids and developed what I thought was an absolutely clear perception of what was going on. Then Kathi would provide another perspective that totally changed everything. And she was right!

After many such experiences, I've wondered, *How do single parents do this with nobody around to give them some depth perception?*

You have that restriction. You must deal with three-dimensional problems with an eye missing. Without another opinion, you have only your severely restricted gaze to rely on.

Then comes the issue of noticing patterns. I've never been good at noticing patterns in my kids. But Kathi is great at this. Several years ago, our daughter, Jessie, was getting tired a lot. She was running track, taking baton lessons, staying active in youth group, and doing great in school.

Seemed to me she needed to go to bed earlier. When that failed and she was still tired, I thought she had mono.

Kathi noticed something different. From her vantage point the problem was sugar. She noticed that whenever Jessie drank pop or ate simple carbohydrates, she got tired. Her remedy was to eliminate sugar. Jess perked right up and was fine thereafter.

Patterns. Finding them all by yourself is hard. Don't panic. Stay cool; admit that one of your eyes is gone. Perhaps you should seek out an honest person to provide another perspective. Pick a tough parent of a teen, a friend you can trust for cheerful, bold, and constructive truth-telling. You need the truth, and you need it in large doses.

Power-of-One Rule 2:
Negotiate with Your Saboteurs

Life is hard enough without an ex-spouse or your in-laws making your life more difficult. Almost everybody has a horror story about this. Many of us face human beings who want nothing more than to see us fail. And they do whatever they can to push our failure along.

I'm going to make some suggestions that will help ease the antics of saboteurs. But handling saboteurs is something you must be ever vigilant in. This is tough, and there aren't many guidelines for you to follow that will work in every case. Remember, however, that most saboteurs don't want to punish the kids. It's you they're after. Kids are simply the weapon of choice.

Call a meeting with your saboteur for the express purpose of negotiating a temporary cease-fire. The reason these meetings often fail is because there's no clear agenda. Be brief, be organized, and be clear. Specify those items you want addressed (no-shows on days they're to spend with the kids, procrastination on returning the kids, late support payments, direct and hostile criticism of you and your decisions, bad-mouthing you in front of the kids, etc.). Temporary fixes often turn into habits permanent enough to live with.

Another saboteur could be your son himself. No anger is worse than anger directed at yourself. Your son probably feels somewhat responsible for your marital situation or other chronic family problems you face—and he's most likely angry at himself over it. As strange as it sounds, it's quite common for people committed to hating themselves to obstruct any effort to improve matters. On the surface he may look like a nasty impediment to progress when on the inside he really just hates himself. Consider this possibility in all dealings with your son.

Follow the rule that if you have a problem or hunch about a problem, get it on the conversation table as quickly as you can. Talking about it, even briefly, can create great dividends for long-term peace.

Power-of-One Rule 3: Get Some Cross-Gender Insights

One of the greatest needs for parents under pressure is to get some cross-gender insights. We all understand the teen version of our own gender. We lived it. We remember it. But understanding the opposite gender? That's what spouses are for!

So if you're a single mom, how are you supposed to understand teenage men? You can't, at least not as well as you need to. But remember two things: First, so what? Just because your teenage son is hard to understand doesn't mean there aren't things you can do. Understanding things from his perspective would be great and helpful, but don't think you're ruined because you don't have it. Just because you don't have perfect understanding doesn't mean you're beyond help. Yes, better understanding makes for better fixes, but in the meantime there are scads of things you can do.

Second, unless you live in a convent, half the people you know are probably men. They've been there. You don't need to be married to get a fair glimpse into the world of teenage men. Ask men for ideas on anything from toilet habits to dressing, dating, driving, shaving, and diet.

Stressed for Success: Making Your Own Good News

What are successful but stressed parents doing? Long ago I did sports-performance consulting. I worked with high-performance athletes to get their heads working well. These people work in what I would call high-pressure atmospheres. I learned a lot. In working with parents under pressure, I've noticed them naturally doing what performance athletes do. You'll notice the principles of provocative parenting in the following list. A provocative parent isn't a captive of any circumstance. Rather, a provocative parent sorts through the resources at hand and finds a way to *make good things happen.* For example:

- Separate your pain from the challenges you face.
- Simplify what you want to accomplish.
- Force yourself to be flexible.
- Be honest.
- Get input.
- Laugh a lot.

Now let's look at these suggestions one by one.

Separate Your Pain from the Challenges You Face

Most singles are riddled by guilt and pain over how things have turned out. They feel bad that they can't give their kids what they believe the kids need. They feel even worse that another adult isn't around to help shoulder all the responsibilities that need to be handled. Their pain can be deep.

To handle this, many single parents have to leave their pain behind them. They have to separate themselves from their pain and move on to face their challenges. Parents who carry deep disappointments or unmet expectations of all kinds face the same hurdle.

Perhaps this is the next step for you. To the extent you can, try to see this day as the first in a long series of individual days. Take a moment right now to think about what's happened just today. Think about events on their own merit, not clouded with the regrets of yesterday or the vague terrors of tomorrow. Just consider today, without any other baggage.

This simple exercise usually begins to lift pressure. Today's troubles somehow don't seem quite so bad. What's over is over, and the only move you should care about is the next one. God has used all the pressure in your life to fill you with much wisdom, and it's in your next move that all that wisdom becomes alive and useful to others. You may be more useful now as a result of your pain than you ever were before without it.

Also, resist the very human urge to compare your home life to others with lower-stress households. You only inflate the pressure on yourself by demanding that your home and kids be as nice—as quiet, as "acceptable," or whatever—as the Joneses', when in fact it just can't be. Not now anyway.

Simplify What You Want to Accomplish

There's no longer the time or resources available to accomplish what you had once hoped to do. But not all is lost. Instead of deciding you're a loser, choose to be a "possibility parent" and adopt a new measure of success.

I know successful single dads and moms who boil down what they want into more simple desires: having a meaningful conversation with their son once a week, supporting their teenager in one area of his interest with enthusiasm and cooperation, or making Sunday count. Their mission becomes more focused on doable goals than on big, glorious dreams. Perhaps you can relate to the woman who told me that she will have met her goal with her son if she can still speak to him after his teenage years!

I hope you won't have to boil down your goals that far. But take some time to focus on the simple things you can do. You may not be able to bike across Europe with your son before he leaves the nest. But you can determine to take three shorter trips of three hours apiece. If you're a noncustodial parent, you won't be able to give him a good-night hug as often as you'd like. But you can make sure he's in no doubt whatsoever about how much you want to.

Knowing what you want to do, no matter how simple, and then realizing those objectives is the key to feeling that you've been successful. It's not the size of the goal that brings you parental satisfaction; it's accomplishing it. Slim down and succeed.

Force Yourself to Be Flexible

Successful overstressed parents of teenage boys understand that to win they must be flexible. Rigidity will snap them into splinters. The teenage years are a messy, error-prone business under the best circumstances. The only way stressed parents can survive those years with their health and happiness intact is to stop expecting perfection and learn to bend.

A Closer Focus

Vacation Plans

As your son moves into adolescence, he stops indulging your parental nostalgia for the family that used to be. Vacations can turn into war zones. If you're not careful, what's intended for fun can end up hurting.

Let go of what used to work. Let go of what's *supposed* to be family fun. Ask him what kind of family play would interest him. Do your best to play together. Remember, these teenage years are a season.

Let him bring along a friend.

Or vacation alone this year. You'll still be a good parent.

How do you do this? Start your training with something about your son that bothers you just a little bit. Maybe it's one of his silly mannerisms or some other essentially harmless activity. Then make yourself like it—and look forward to it!

Next, make a short list of big bothers, such as:

- dress
- music
- room decor
- lessons or other extracurricular activities

Ask yourself what will matter in twenty years. Ask where his preferences and your pride might be getting mixed up. You may have more room to create flexibility in yourself than you imagined.

This is not fun, so don't get your hopes up. Sometimes I don't like bending either. Nobody does. But make yourself bend and flex on something simple now and then, and live to fight really important battles another day. It may not be what you want right now, but it's smart, and the bend-training will pay off big.

Be Honest

Honesty with others is the only policy for single parents. It's a great stress reliever. I know so many new single parents who are afraid to discuss the grit of their kid troubles because they're embarrassed.

Seasoned players know the virtue in just letting the awful truth hang out. It's amazing what can germinate from the fertile left-behinds of a bad experience.

Within intact marriages and other flavors of average families, hiding weaknesses and warts is easier. It's expected. Pressured parents don't have that luxury, so if you're one of them, I urge you to stop your hiding right now. Do it for the sake of expediency. You'll have to come clean anyway. And in the long run it's better for your mental health.

Get Input

Closely associated with honesty is getting input from others. I suggest several sources: your son, experienced individuals, and a team of your creation. Talking directly to your son may be your best source of information on rearing him. In chapter 5, "Stealth Communication," I'll tell you more about how to do this, but I'll mention one thing here. Most young men cannot help but help those who need help. Read that again slowly. They want to be of value, and they will be if you ask them for help. They experience the difficulty of your situation just as intensely as you, and they feel somewhat responsible.

He's actually looking for ways he can be of help, but you need to show him in a way that he can positively respond. Sometimes the words "I need your help," spoken softly, have a remarkable effect. Don't say them until you are clear exactly what you need. State it positively: "I need you to be home when we agree you'll be home," instead of, "Why do you always need to be late?" Clarify the specific, positive thing you need. Then proceed. For most young men, this works to a very productive and satisfying end.

Find an older, experienced parent to whom you can air yourself out from time to time. If you haven't one of these older folks in your life, you're missing some of the best help around.

These folks are almost always willing to help, and they are networked with other helpful singles. Look for parents of both genders who have sons the same age as yours. Try to find positive ones; many singles are bitter and have a caustic "us against the world" attitude that will poison you. Steer clear of those folks. Find, search out, and develop a give-and-take relationship with a small group of positive parents who understand your special needs.

Take this even one step further. I've met many successful single parents of sons who have a tight support group consisting of three to five people. This isn't a social group but a team. They've made a specific commitment to one another. It's not casual. You will be blessed to have such a group of dedicated individuals on your side. The ideas and opinions available from such a group could be better than the input you'd get in a marriage.

Create a blend of people devoted to making sure you succeed. Be the initiator. Right now, there are others out there, parents just like you, looking for this kind of support team.

Laugh a Lot!

So life blew up on you. You've experienced some of the worst pain a human can endure. All your fine dreams have been blown to dust. Your son's dreams too. You're both upset at yourselves and the world. It's hard to predict how your son will respond to all this. But I recommend you do one thing soon.

Laugh. Laugh hard. You're still here, and life is still moving on. God has given you a new opportunity. There is something about that worth howling about. It's OK. Go ahead.

Remember that any home can be a happy home. It's about attitude. Your son may remember when you were stressed and depressed; he may remember that time he came home to an empty house that his dad just left. You can't stop that. But if he remembers his mom joking with him or laughing a lot or making *Jeopardy* into a contest each night—those memories will serve as great buffers.

What Could God Possibly Have for Me?

God gave you your son because He knew that, come what may, you'd pursue the best possible course for him. Married or single, troubles will come. Your heart is with your son, and your heart for God will transcend your troubles. God will find a way to bless your efforts. He always does—that's why His name is Redeemer. He can turn *any* circumstance or problem to good. Ask for His blessing boldly, and expect it forthrightly. God likes our confidence in Him.

Not long ago I saw a great "thinking of you" card. On it was a steadily rising graph line with the numbers one to thirty printed across the bottom. The rising line abruptly dipped to the bottom of the graph over the numbers fourteen to sixteen then rose slowly again off to the right. The caption of the card was the title of the graph: "A parent's impact over the years." As a result of reading this book, your long-term impact on your son is going to rise.

What you see now may be obstacles. What will remain over time is your profound presence in your son's life.

PART TWO

SHAPING THE INNER MAN AT HOME

Chapter Five

Stealth
Communication

*Slipping through your son's invisible lines of defense
(to connect with his heart)*

Not long ago my brother-in-law Matt and my son Jake were hiking behind me on a wooded trail. We'd been traveling for a long time, and they were carrying on an animated conversation about art, philosophy, spirituality, and women. I wanted desperately to jump in, because something very special was happening. Jake was talking openly. A lot! I hiked ahead, carefully collecting and savoring every word.

As I walked along, several things hit me. First, I knew if I spoke up it would surely wreck the moment. The reason he was talking was because I wasn't! Second, he was saying things that amazed me. The depth of his responses and the sharpness of his questions really impressed me. It was a delightful surprise.

But what stood out most was the fact that Matt was connecting with my kid. Matt was like an F-117 Stealth pilot on a reconnaissance mission. He'd slipped in under the defenses and was systematically exploring what was, for me, forbidden territory. He'd connected with Jake in a way I rarely experience. *Why can't I do that?* I wondered. *Am I a dope or a bore?*

Perhaps you've asked yourself similar questions: *Why is it so hard to get my son to talk to me about things that matter?*

Isn't that what all of us as parents crave? Sure, we want to communicate our beliefs and opinions to our sons. But most of all, we want to figure out how to make connections that affect their inner core, how to penetrate our sons' invisible defenses.

Sometimes the problem is us. We don't know how to approach our sons and get them to open up. What we need is a whole new vocabulary. And we need to understand better just what the "defense code" means.

Code Rules for Teen Talk

Let's start with a provocative question: *If your son could talk about talking, what would he tell you?* You would probably hear some statements like these:

"Talking is hard work. If I'm not comfortable, I won't risk it." Our teens are much more uncomfortable with us than we are with them. We have much more experience in talking—thirty to fifty years' experience in most cases. Teens aren't as sophisticated with the tools. They don't yet know how to put feelings into verbal expressions and thoughts into strings of intelligible sentences. They're just coasting between some phase in their life and are just too fogged to have anything to say. All this adds up to a conversational cocktail that can be as flat as water.

"Don't mistake me for someone who shares your interests." As a mature adult, you've already developed your favorite ways of talking and interacting. You've made decisions about the topics you enjoy discussing, the information you like getting, and the pace at which you like conversing. These don't mesh with what your son enjoys. What interests you probably doesn't interest him. This goes for both the potential topics you have to discuss and the way in which you do it.

If anyone is to adjust in this situation it must be you. Your son is still sorting ideas, arranging prejudices, testing styles, and making decisions about everything. And based upon some of the realities we've discussed about the nature of teenagers, you can be pretty sure he's not going to want to be identical to you even if he could.

"I feel less pressured talking with adults who aren't my parents." Teens often love to talk with other adults yet aren't that impressed with parental interest. In your presence your son feels parental pressure, yet in the presence of other adults he senses a bit more freedom. He has no personal history with that adult, so he interacts with ease. And when he talks to another adult, he doesn't have to worry about consequences.

A Closer Focus

The Story on Self-Esteem

The current emphasis on getting "raised on praise" leaves some kids with the attitude that praise is better than performance. But I want to challenge you as a parent to praise less and demand more.

Real self-esteem happens inside kids when they learn they can actually overcome an obstacle and do things—it's built one brick at a time by a process of victory and defeat. In most situations, your son knows very well whether he's done a good job. You can teach him to rise to an occasion and perform at his peak. But blindly shelling out platitudes won't make him strong inside.

Confidence comes from knowing, not just talking. Confidence comes from *competence*, not from persuasion. If, in a loving and accepting relationship, you encourage your son to focus on skill building, confidence *will* come.

I saw this mismatch of expectations in my counseling practice all the time. When I worked with whole families together, I could quickly pry kids open in front of their parents. Getting them to talk was a breeze. Parents showered me with thanks. But the counselor is neutral, safe, and skilled—a huge advantage.

"I'll talk when I'm ready—not when you want me to." Sometimes teens will suddenly, for no apparent reason, open up. It always surprises me when they get chatty, and as far as I can tell it surprises them too. Teenagers surprise themselves in many ways! It's almost as if for brief moments their strong sense of privacy relaxes and they can converse freely, without pressure or force.

We adults, on the other hand, can pretty much talk on command. We take it for granted and can mistakenly insist on it from our teens. Pushing like that usually doesn't work. Timing is everything. Respect it. Make time work for you—and realize that it's usually a waste to push when the door says "pull."

Talking isn't necessarily communication, just like putting flour in the oven isn't necessarily baking. Real communication is much more mysterious and powerful than getting words out. Words are just the beginning.

More Than Words Can Say

All communication between people boils down to sending (speaking, writing, snarling, smiling) and receiving (listening, perceiving, interpreting). Successful communication is measured by what's accurately understood, and failure is measured by what's missed.

In sending and receiving, two dimensions are at work—what's communicated by words and what's communicated by our body, tone, and facial expressions. These two, verbal and nonverbal interaction, create an intricate web of subtlety and power.

The influence we possess by properly utilizing these two dimensions—verbal and nonverbal—is staggering. Yet most of us are ignorant of word strength and even worse about nonverbal connections.

To connect with your son, understand that everything you say can be said better. Every movement you make has impact on your listener. Every glance you shoot conveys meaning. Learn how to manage these verbal and nonverbal channels with loving skill, and a whole new territory of communication with your teenager will open up.

Research indicates that at least 55 percent of communication is physiological (how you sit, squirm, look), 38 percent is tonal (how you sound), and only 7 percent is actually the words you use. That means that roughly 93 percent of everything you communicate has nothing to do with what you say.

When I wanted to test out those findings for myself, I did an experiment on my kids. I made five statements with my mouth, then directly contradicted those statements with my actions. Then I watched and listened to my kids carefully to see which they believed. You can try this. Here are a few examples. I said:

- "Bill Clinton is a great president" as I shook my head *no* violently.
- "Would you please come here and give me a hug?" as I pushed them away.
- "Let's get this room cleaned up" as I sauntered around, throwing things on the floor.
- "I really do trust you, honey" as I looked down my nose and shook my head slyly.

In every case, they first reacted with confusion. Then they believed my actions, not my mouth.

So what are you communicating nonverbally? Don't be embarrassed if you don't have a clue. Not only are we in the dark about what we're communicating, but often we know even less about how to take advantage of this skill.

Sending effective nonverbals is mainly about *coherence*. Coherence means matching your words with your actions. You gain tremendous credibility and impact when you consciously match your bodily actions with your words. For instance, if you want to say "I love you" in a powerful way, create body actions and expressions that clearly match:

- Sit forward
- Look intently
- Make concerted eye contact
- Speak up
- Put some heart into it

The amazing truth is that if you do nothing more than consciously make your body match what your brain is saying or thinking, your communication ability will skyrocket.

Does everyone interpret body language the same way? Yes and no. The signals our body sends are fairly universal. But the differences in how we interpret both verbal and nonverbal communication have to do with how we process and receive our information.

I See What You're Saying:
Identifying Your Son's Favorite Communication Pattern

Every person has a favorite "sense" they rely on to send and receive information with other people. For example, people favoring the sense of sight use visual references when they talk—"I see what you mean," or

"That's clear to me," or "Show me more." People who favor hearing use auditory references, such as "I hear what you're saying," or "That sounds good to me," or "Tell me more." Those who favor their feelings use kinesthetic references, such as "I can feel what you're saying," or "That feels like a fit to me," or "Can you press that out for me a little more?" (Not many people favor smelling or tasting. And don't stand too close if they do.)

You can have some fun with this by asking your son to describe a moment of his day in detail. Rather than asking how his day went, ask him what he did, say, between sixth and seventh period, in detail. As he describes this, notice what "sense" words he uses the most. Does he tell you how things looked, how they sounded, or how it all felt? Obviously this requires that you spend some time observing your son in ways that may be new to you. But focus the best you can.

If you watch him carefully, more patterns emerge. You'll notice that whenever he's creating pictures in his mind or visualizing, he'll look up and may even throw his shoulders back slightly. If he's feeling something deeply, he'll tend to look down and slump his shoulders forward.

A Closer Focus

Introducing Mr. Hyde

Your son is probably not aware of how his behavior and attitudes bounce up and down. He needs your help to see himself accurately. To illustrate to your boy what's really going on in his mood swings, leave a tape recorder on during chore times, dinner, preparation for school in the morning, or any other time when Mr. Hyde shows himself. When you replay it with him in private—to inform, not to insult him—your son will be hearing himself in a whole new light.

If he's remembering something he heard, he'll glance side to side as if he's listening. This is gilded, nonverbal information he doesn't even know he's showing you. Discipline yourself to notice it.

If you ask him about a girl and he glances up and tilts his head back, he's seeing her. If he rolls his eyes sideways and swivels his head, he's probably hearing the sound of her voice. If he looks down, he's feeling something. With just a little effort you'll notice if he prefers his visual, auditory, or kinesthetic sense most of the time.

This is all very reliable. Knowing your son's favorite sensory system puts you in spectacular position to read him nonverbally and connect more successfully. You can now help build rapport with your son by matching your own movements and language to his. This doesn't mean that you copy or mimic him. It means that you generally assume the same body posture, pace, and tone he uses.

You'll do your son and yourself a big favor if you try as much as possible to communicate in his preferred way:

If he's visual: You know your son is visual if he looks up often, talks rather rapidly, and uses higher inflections, almost following his upward eye sweeps.

How might such a kid like to be approached? When you speak, look up occasionally, especially at times when things are tense or at an impasse. Speak rapidly from time to time. Use visual words such as "I see what you mean," or "That looks like something I'd do," or "I can see your point," or "That's real clear." Whenever possible, spice your discussions with visual aids and stimuli, such as a magazine article; if there's nothing to look at, use word pictures and metaphors. Try to be descriptive in your words, using colors or images. Approach topics as often as possible from the standpoint of how they look or appear.

If he's auditory: If your son is auditory, keep your voice tones even and your volume set to match his. Match his tempo and rhythm. Sit in the same position and be very aware of your tones and direction of your voice as you speak. Use auditory references like "I hear you," or "That rings true for me," or "That sounds good to me."

If he's auditory, he will probably respond better to a taped message from you than a letter. He will also take more in by hearing repeated phrases than other kids will. He will hear you better and think you are really hearing him. He'll say to himself, "Hey, this person is really listening to what I say."

If he's kinesthetic (feeling-oriented): If your son is kinesthetic, assume the same sitting or standing position he does. Try to speak softly, quietly, and at whatever pace he sets. Occasionally touch him casually and warm the conversation as much as you can. Ask him how he feels versus what he thinks, and use your own feelings to communicate ideas whenever possible. You can gradually equip him with words to express his feelings by using them yourself. Try to be specific, and use words that go way past happy or sad: blissful, melancholy, weary, thrilled, moody, vulnerable, fragile, nervous, afraid, intimidated, insecure.

If you use these techniques, not only will you communicate better, but you will observe your son much more carefully, and he'll know it. That'll impress him. And on your end, your sensory awareness will shoot up, enabling you to see repeating patterns, to understand your son's signals, and to begin to penetrate past defenses into that uncharted territory where you can really make a connection.

In short, you'll become excellent at both your verbal and nonverbal communication. But those are only the mechanics. Now it's time to delve into what it takes to send and receive great information across the wonderful bridge you've built.

Now We're Communicating

I hope you have a greater appreciation for the power you can generate by harnessing nonverbal elements of human interaction. For parents, knowing how to turbocharge your talk is vital.

Most of us have been taught that to be a good communicator we must be clear, direct, succinct, honest, and forthright. That's all true. But a key principle is often left out: *It is our job to assume full responsibility for what our kids are hearing.* This is a huge leap from what most of us have been taught about communication. It puts the entire burden of communication solely on the speaker, not on the hearer. In other words, the meaning of your communication is the response you get.

The premise is simple. Because we have different agendas and worldviews, our communication is bound to miss occasionally in the transmission. You can carry on what appears to be a completely successful conversation yet have each person walk away with wildly different interpretations of what occurred.

This happened in our house at report-card time. After looking over the grades and carrying on a brief, lighthearted conversation with the kids, they often thought Kathi and I were picking on them. Somehow our messages of encouragement and support sounded shrill and demeaning to them.

This is a great example of the kind of cross-up that goes on in small ways all the time with teenage boys. Never mind that maybe they're having a bad day or that they're misunderstood or that they're being unfair. Those issues are irrelevant to the person who is committed to being a powerful communicator.

Within this mind-set, the hearer, rather than the speaker's agenda, becomes the point of reference. Think about what a profound shift in perspective this is. I've been utterly shocked at how empowered my communication has become by adhering to this principle. No longer do I find myself whining, "But you just don't understand me," or "That's not what I meant." Now I assume total and full responsibility to make myself clear, reliable, and understandable.

Pretty soon you'll be doing the same thing.

Get Good at Questions

I know, I know, he won't answer your questions. Is there anything more typical than a teenager with a one-syllable grunt in response to every inquiry? Their silence drives us wild. No wonder we're tempted to become mind readers and buy crystal balls!

Unfortunately, mind reading can backfire pretty badly with teenagers. I suggest that rather than assume you know what's happening inside your son's head, you take some time and ask some great questions. And since all questions are not created equal, here are some tips on honing your skills— all of which revolve around the idea of assuming responsibility for change.

Be specific. If you pay attention you'll learn that in many cases vague answers are born from vague questions. If you ask a vague question like, "How was your day?" a vague reply works fine. Actually a grunt will work fine, too, and that's often all you get!

Teenagers always give vague answers to vague questions but might give specific answers to specific questions! One key to good questions is to never ask anything that can be answered yes or no. Start your questions with, "Tell me…," or "How…," or "What…"

If you ask a specific question and still get mush, try saying, "Tell me specifically," or "What specifically do you mean?" The results can be surprising.

"How was your day, dear?"

"Huu bluuu huu huu."

"What specifically do you mean?"

"Huh?"

"What specifically do you mean it was 'Huu bluuu huu huu'?"

"It was fine, Mom."

"What specifically do you mean by it was fine?"

"Mom, are you reading that teenager book again?"

"What specifically do you mean by reading?"

Disarm your inquiry. Being rather new to all this communication business, teenage boys are often not sure how they should reply. To them, our questions don't represent a caring request for information but something closer to a "test" or a scourging that they might fail at. They handle the momentary confusion by saying nothing.

This is especially true when it comes to our favorite question: "Why?" The "why" question creates enormous defensiveness because the implied message is *Defend what you've done.* So they either defend themselves or go silent.

So how can you disarm your questions? Just talk about the intent of your question. Say, "I know you might think I'm prying by asking

---

A Closer Focus

Laugh It Up

One rule of stealth communication says, "If you can make them laugh, you own 'em." If you don't know any jokes, go find some (at the library, funny friends, Jay Leno). Prior to or during a serious conversation, interject your humorous story, quip, or joke at a moment when it might fit. Or tell a humorous story on yourself. Humor will change the openness of your boy because it places you in a radically different role and helps your son experience you from a fresh perspective.

you about your day, but I don't know how to ask it without sounding like the Gestapo. Sorry! I just love you. So how was your day?" Such words will often make your son relax a bit and tell you what's up.

Persist and experiment. There are no one-shot deals with kids. Throughout your life with your son, you'll find many "inspired moments" when you will connect and be close. Should an opportunity fade or slip by, don't despair. More are on the way.

That's why I urge you to experiment, especially with thought-provoking questions. Teenagers are like cats: They like to maintain their balance and land on their feet. But if they're always comfortable, they're likely to be napping. Crazy or surprising questions keep them interested.

You can think them up yourself or steal them from magazines, books, or conversations you hear at work:

- "Do you think they should execute murderers?"
- "Of all the diseases in the world, which would you least like to get and why?"
- "I heard a speaker who said that if you can name the top three things you think will happen to you today, they will happen. What are your three?"

Too often the reason teenagers get quiet with us is because our questions don't wake them up. They can see us and our humdrum agenda coming a hundred miles away.

Provoke Conversations

Let's take all this a step further. The best conversations are those that happen naturally. But why wait? In the absence of these, you can "provoke" conversations with great results:

Choose a provocative venue. If you're an attentive communicator, you'll notice quickly that getting rapport with your son is easier in some places than in others. Laid back in his bedroom works better than seated around the dining room table for a drilling session under a heat lamp. Driving in a car is better than face-offs in front of the school.

Some venues are surefire failures! I've found that it's useless to have a Ward Clever talk with Wally in our living room. Somehow that place has become poisoned territory for heavy conversations. The place to provoke conversation easiest is often in the car. Wally talks when we cruise with some tunes, wind in our hair and heavy words spoken from the heart.

Talk while you're having fun. By accident I learned that, to teenage boys, talking is something you do while you're having fun. Once a group of boys was at our house, basically being bored. I threw out a few suggestions. They haughtily machine-gunned every one.

I went out and started shooting baskets by myself. To my surprise, within minutes the gang came out and joined me. What amazed me most was that as soon as they entered the court, they wouldn't stop talking. They were so open during the game that they answered questions about their families, girl problems, and money woes.

I actually thought for a minute that I'd invented a new kind of therapy: basketball analysis! Rather than weave baskets, we'd shoot 'em! What I'd actually done is discover something that great communicators have known for a long time: Teenagers never discuss things. Talking is something you do while you're having fun.

If you want to provoke great conversations with your teen, get in the habit of conducting them while you're doing something else. If you sit him down on your *Father Knows Best* couch, your conversation will be a guaranteed flop. Instead find something interesting to do—and while you're at it, talk.

Reveal something surprising. A special feeling overcomes me when I share something with my teenagers that makes their jaws drop open. Why? *I'm making something happen.* For better or worse, our kids stereotype us. They've already made judgments about us, how we think and how we act. In most cases their judgments of us are right on target. Disturbingly so. The problem is this: When they can stereotype us to their satisfaction, it's an easy step for them to dismiss us as predictable.

Making jaw-dropping statements cures that problem. We see this ably modeled by Jesus. On just about every page of the Gospels, Jesus delivers at least one jaw-dropper:

- "I did not come to bring peace, but a sword" (Matthew 10:34).
- "The last will be first, and the first will be last" (Matthew 20:16).
- "Therefore be wise as serpents and harmless as doves" (Matthew 10:16, NKJV).
- "Whoever loses his life for me will find it" (Matthew 16:25).

Jesus made truth a dramatic event and was strategic in the way He presented it to listeners.

Saying something controversial or unpredictable forces your teenager to assess you and deal with you. What could you say?

- "I think about sex every day." *(Gee, Dad, I thought you were too old for that.)*
- "I sense that God has been telling me something very important about you, son." *(Um, OK, Mom, what is it?)*
- "I'd like to hitchhike across the states next summer. *(Yeah, right. That crazy stuff is for kids…Hey, can I come?)*

You can't be so easily stereotyped when you throw away the "I'm the parent" script and reveal the human, maybe slightly frayed, part of yourself.

Say More with Less

Out of a one-thousand-word lecture (which is pretty average), how many words do you think your teenager actually hears? Your guess is probably as low as mine. (Ask him sometime to repeat what you've said in casual conversation then judge for yourself what he might hear when he's really mad at you.) When you speak, you have more impact when you say it in as few words as possible. In almost all situations, you can think carefully about what you wish to say then boil it down to a short, punchy statement. You'll need to practice, because most of us warm to our subject—we say what we mean to say in five or six ways, trying to improve with each try—but by the time we get there, our audience is dead cold.

And then there's the virtue of simply listening. Listening will do more to improve the relationship between you and your son than anything you could say. Do you really want to connect with power? Then listen. Do you really want to be heard? Then hush. Do you really want your boy to remember your words? Then pipe down.

Young guys want to be all right but don't always know what all right is. They can't always divulge true motives, fears, and pains because they aren't always sure what they are. So just listen to them. Let them be wrong, feel wrong, say it wrong—really off track—and if necessary, let them be wrong for a long time. Risk this radical communication idea: *Your son's freedom to try and fail to communicate to you about himself and his world is more important than your ability to communicate brilliantly back to him.*

So listen without speaking. Just listen.

Vary Your Forms of Communication

Write a letter. Letter writing is one of the most powerful and neglected means of communication. Think about this: If your son is highly visual, he'll be able to see what you're saying by virtue of words and paper. If he's auditory, he'll talk to himself in your voice as he reads your words. If he's kinesthetic, he'll have something to hang on to. This is a marvelous means to connect with accuracy and specificity.

I'm often asked what parents should write about. I suggest you write letters about anything that interests you. If you have a problem or a concern, encouragement, praise, or condemnation, written words are a great way to convey the message. Pictures work well, too, as do cartoons, poems, jokes, and stories. You can deliver the letters in person, hide them under his pillow, stick them in his lunch, or mail them. Be wild! Be creative!

And don't be concerned if he doesn't read them. He will. Eventually the curiosity will get him. Will it connect? Of course it will. When he's ready.

Write a poem or a song lyric. You don't need to be Longfellow or McCartney here. He'll think you're nuts, but my bet is that he won't throw your poetry away.

Read a book together. This is a great way to spur conversations. It's powerful and easy to try. The easiest way to do this is to find out what books he must read for school and ask him for permission to read it with him. In almost every case he'll be delighted to share the misery with someone. The conversations coming from those shared journeys will be well worth the homework.

Share a movie together. Combine your desire to spend time with him and his interest in tubs of popcorn. It's almost a ritual these days to go to movies, and doing it together for the purpose of finding discussion topics is brilliant. Let Spielberg or Cruise or De Niro roll out your conversations on the big screen. Everything's there: characters in conflict, morals (and amorals) on display, teenagers making big and small choices, consequences convincingly demonstrated, great art to be appreciated, lousy exploitations to be trashed… If you do it together, you'll be building an inventory of commonalities to spur conversations for the rest of your lives.

"We Were Still Talking…"

A friend of mine recently told me some reassuring news. We were talking about hearing underneath our sons' intellect and hearing their emotions and hearts. I was particularly interested in this guy, because his son had been the classic bad apple. His teenage years were a rap sheet of trouble. Name it, and he'd stung his dad with it.

The good news was that the young man, now twenty-four years old, had returned three times in the last year for advice!

"What's the secret?" I begged.

"By the grace of God," the father said, "we were still talking by the time he grew up."

Hang in there, folks. You may be on the dark side of the moon in this communication business, but soon there will be a son rise.

Chapter Six

Too Big to Spank

Mastering the mysteries of teen discipline

I can be an intense, impatient, even bossy person. I'm really working, however, on controlling those qualities. That's why I agreed to let my kids get a dog. I figured it'd be good training.

It was training, all right! I didn't understand what I was getting myself into. I wasn't raised with dogs, so I thought they'd be much smarter. The only "animals" I was raised with were two brothers and two sisters. They could do dishes, leave when I wanted them to, clean up their own messes, help with homework, and loan me money. Man's best friend can't do any of those things.

Dogs do learn, but way too slowly for me. I learned that when you're dealing with a canine you must keep it simple, use treats, don't expect miracles right off the bat, and don't ever try to outthink them. Thinking from a dog's perspective will leave you scratching your head with your foot.

Forgive the awkward transition here, but attempting to change the behavior of a teenage boy can be surprisingly similar. Trying to unscramble your son's logic and motivations and get him to behave in a certain way can leave you wishing you could just put in a call to the obedience trainer.

Discipline is always about shaping behavior, not about punishment. It's about making life better for everybody, not just for Mom and Dad. For our sons, the purpose of discipline goes beyond getting a quick response to a command.

- We want to influence behavior and the decision making that goes with it.
- We want to shape inner convictions, character qualities, whole futures.
- We want them to take positive outer controls and make them their own.

An adult, after all, is someone who's taken the influences and controls of childhood and turned them into personal advantages in life.

This process of training for maturity will seem slow, confusing, and frustrating. But the boys at my house and yours show incredible promise. Discipline might look like it's all about holding him back (he'll certainly complain about leashes and muzzles and such). But don't be fooled. The aim of smart discipline is to nurture a better person—and a happier one too.

That makes learning the art worth every ounce of pain and effort required.

A Sore Subject

Pain and discipline seem to go together—and I'm not referring to how the kids experience it. Discipline is a disturbing topic for most parents. When the subject comes up in parenting seminars, I brace myself for heated remarks:

- "I've tried everything! Being firm. Being a friend. I'm ready to give up!"
- "We both work full time, and I don't have the time or energy to discipline my teens the way my parents disciplined me!"
- "How do I control what my teen does when he's bigger than I am, spends most of his time somewhere else, and he ignores the discipline I do hand out?"
- "I think I messed up early on. My teen doesn't respect me. Isn't it too late? Shouldn't I just find a way to hang on for dear life until it's over?"

Don't give up so easily. You have options.

Though our society has cycled through many kinds of child-rearing fads, teenage boys haven't changed at all. They aren't bad, but they do occasionally lie, cheat, hide, and sneak. That's all pretty common stuff. It's time to start treating them with appropriate clear-eyed realism.

Moving from Fear to Opportunity

Can you handle the truth? The truth is that your son has many faces. He only shows you what he wants you to see. You don't know your son as well as you might think, no matter how good your relationship is. You must handle this multifaced kid and the troubles he presents with care.

The penalty you face if you don't handle these problems well can paralyze you with fear. You fear scrapes with the law, poor academic performance, unemployability, getting a girl pregnant, substance abuse, car crashes, and more.

But your opportunity here is significant. You have the opportunity to make his adolescence a time of great learning and growth, to prepare him for all the challenges that come with adulthood. Sound discipline starts with putting down our fears—or, as we'll see, choosing a better fear—and facing the truth about our sons.

Discipline means handling natural tendencies. As I mentioned in chapter 2, the most profound tendencies in a teenage boy are pleasure, pain, and curiosity. Self-discipline for boys means postponing pleasure, enduring pain, and controlling their curiosities. All discipline coming from you boils down to taking action to change your son's natural forces.

This is where the problem of discipline enters. We laud those who can discipline themselves to do hard things. But disciplining others? That's another matter. Entire books are available on the topic. The current opinions about disciplining others, especially kids, is a gangly octopus of ideas and contradictions. You've probably noticed the huge gap between the discipline we *know* works and the discipline we're *told* works.

We've all experienced discipline from the other side and understand it in our own way. We know how it works, how it fails, what's effective, and how it's best applied. Let's try to sort this out.

We've Made a Trade

We're one of the first generations in history that thinks raising kids is hard. We're also one of the first generations obsessed with getting it right and with being perfect parents. As a result, we've made some poor trade-offs in the way we handle our kids. In short, we've traded discipline *that works* for discipline that *sounds good*.

Rigid conduct codes, strict obedience, and even spanking used to be considered normal and natural. The popular opinion today is that these methods are cruel and ineffective. They sound bad, thus we seem to conclude immediately they are bad. (I understand why many parents worry that spanking is dangerous. In some cases it might be. But the point is that whether spanking actually works is independent of how it sounds.)

What sounds good today is changing behavior by building self-esteem, maintaining the integrity of the individual, respecting the integrity of the individual, and allowing a child to determine his or her own reality. We use tactics that sound good without any solid proof that they're better, and our culture's discipline fads swing with pendulum predictability.

To find answers, I've preferred finding great kids and asking them how their parents disciplined them. They've convinced me that strong, occasionally forceful discipline is good and builds happy, respectful kids. In the survey I conducted for this book, 80 percent of the teenage boys secretly admitted they deserved to be disciplined for things they'd done. They're asking for discipline!

Teenage men need more discipline in their lives—and they know it.

Invisible Restraints

We've been taught that *fear* is a bad thing. We've also been taught to have negative associations with the word *discipline*. They just sound bad. Yet biblically, fear is good, and discipline is a sign of love. Solomon wrote in Proverbs that fear of God is the beginning of wisdom. The writer of Hebrews said that only someone who loves others would discipline them. Scripture is always surprising and trendsetting. God is pretty smart.

This is what I mean about choosing a better fear. Wise parents make the right kind of fear work for good in their sons.

The most powerful kind of discipline is invisible. This kind of authority and control comes from establishing *who you are* more than *what you'll do* if a rule is broken. Too many parents are stranded without this kind of strong interpersonal posture. They're trapped between two conflicting fears: fearing their kids and their misbehavior, and fearing handling that misbehavior with tough, no-nonsense authority.

Perhaps they fear that strong discipline will make their kids question their love or perhaps rebel more.

It's easiest to establish this kind of authority when kids are young. Parents who send the message, *I'm the adult, you are the kid, and you will do things because I say so,* have happier, better-adjusted children. If the parents do what they say they'll do in consistent, tough, and loving ways, parental credibility lasts well into the teenage years. Life progresses more or less smoothly because communication and expectations are predictable and clear to everyone involved.

A Closer Focus

The Car Deal

Driving is a privilege for everyone. Whether he owns his own car or uses yours, make the rules as clear and specific as you can: wearing seat belts, speed limits, replacing whatever gas he uses, and agreeing how many people can ride at one time. Be sure that any underage passengers he takes along have permission to ride with him. Your son should be learning car maintenance: oil changes, tune-ups, tire rotations, and other simple procedures.

I recommend clear rules *against* :

- transporting drugs or alcohol (even by one of the passengers)
- drag racing
- off-road stunts
- ear-splitting radio volume
- eating while driving
- allowing underage pals to drive

If he breaks the rules, even in his own car, take his keys and oil up his bike.

It's also best to instill a sense of *self-discipline*. Typically that means teaching a child to do difficult things on his own without constant prodding and force. We want our kids to discipline themselves.

Only self-confident parents have personal credibility and the ability to teach self-discipline. Giving you that self-confidence, no matter how you've raised your son or how you feel about your prospects, is what this chapter is about.

Checking Yourself for Leaks

Someplace along the trail of life, many of us have lost the swashbuckling confidence we had as teenagers. If we could only blend the experience of our years with the daring we used to feel, we'd probably be better disciplinarians. The good news is that you still have a few drops of confidence left, no matter what you've been through. The bad news is that you leak, and the confidence you have left will be drained off unless you find out what's causing the leaks.

Let's check you for confidence-and-credibility leaks. Here are five:

- Do you give yourself proper credit?
- Do you feel unable to touch your son's core?
- Do you judge yourself because of mixed feelings?
- Have you succumbed to a diagnosis?
- Are you arguing your strength away?

Do You Give Yourself Proper Credit?

First, let's do a credit check. Are you worth being heard? *Yes.*

Does your son know it? *No.*

It's the nature of teenage boys to know everything themselves. Not long ago my elder son and I were chatting about whether he was mature and disciplined enough to go to a rock concert alone. He's a typical firstborn—headstrong as a mule. Though he's often wrong about things, he won't take input from a frump like me. He was having a difficult time grasping the idea that there might be something bad about going to rock concerts.

At first his stubbornness made me mad. I thought he was just being difficult. Then the truth hit me: *He really does think he knows all he needs to know.* He was confident he knew who might be there, what they might be doing, and what he might get exposed to. He honestly believed that I was the idiot!

"How can you know so much about all this and I don't?" he challenged.

I tried not to chuckle; really I did.

"Because, Jake," I replied evenly, "forty does not equal fifteen, six-foot-one doesn't equal five-foot-eleven, 190 pounds doesn't equal 150 pounds, wrinkled skin doesn't equal smooth skin, and straight, gray hair isn't wavy and brown! I *earned* what I know; I didn't just learn it."

It was one of those extremely rare moments when I made an eloquent checkmate.

Eloquent or not, you're worth being heard. It's time to begin acting like it. No need to be nasty or bludgeon your boy with authority. Just state the facts with confidence. You don't need to *always* explain what you're doing. You've earned the right to be Mom or Dad.

To help plug your confidence leak, repeat these declarations of authority to yourself.

- "He only sees now. I see then and now."
- "I know my son better than any other human does and probably better than he knows himself."
- "No one has better training and experience to be my son's advocate and protector."

- "God has made me responsible for his upbringing and uniquely prepared me to succeed."
- "I pay the bills here. And even though (like every parent) I've made some mistakes and even though I may be having a terrible day, I'm still the best person for this job!"

Your son needs the benefit of that kind of posture and confidence in you. He won't always accept your authority and self-confidence, but that's not your concern. (You wouldn't accept it either if you were a teen.) But it's your job to be the adult in charge.

Do You Feel Unable to Touch Your Son's Core?

Why we discipline our children changes over time. Understanding our "why" motives for discipline will help us find more confidence. Let me explain. When the kids are young, we discipline mostly to protect, teach, and guide. As they get older, most parents would say they discipline to get their sons to listen and obey. I think the motive is deeper.

Face it. We all want to touch our sons in some significant, lasting way. In chapter 2 we discussed our sons' "core." Remember, their core is their real personality, their conscience dwelling behind the facade and forming the bulk of who they really are. We worry a lot about reaching and affecting this core.

We'll do almost anything to feel as though we've affected our sons there. We try emotional gymnastics to find common ground. We bite our tongues when we'd rather bark. We try to be nice, talkative, and permissive, to set kind and workable rules, or to offer compromise—all to try and touch this inner being. But our best efforts often hit stone walls, crunching our egos, agitating our fears, and turning our frustrations up to a slow boil.

Most of us revert to disciplining our sons in a noble, last-gasp attempt to touch them deeply. Unfortunately, we can't yell their cores out into the open, beat them open with our hands, spank them into availability with a board, or access them with a slap. Cores are coy.

The root of the problem is that we don't know how to draw out a teenage boy's inner core, and *he's actively defending it against hackers like us.* The best approach, the most confidence-building approach, is to use a hunter's mentality: Stake out the place and learn to wait. We know his core is in there, and we know it shows itself occasionally. Our job is to silently, quietly wait until we see the soft underside of his core.

Remember, your son wants communication and connections to happen with you. He just doesn't know how. He certainly doesn't know that a family that sets clear boundaries, values self-control, and doesn't give him everything he wants is the *best* place for his inner self to flourish.

Content yourself to stay in his proximity and trust your parenting plan—and his deepest parts will show up.

A Closer Focus

Keeping Time

Who's responsible to get young Fred to basketball practice? Well, if young Fred is five, probably you are. If Fred is fifteen, well…it's a fine line between letting your son run his own schedule and dealing with missed appointments, letting down other people, ignoring deadlines. A young man needs help—pointers in schedule management, occasional reminders, maybe a ride—but don't steal the responsibility. That's his.

The usefulness of being responsible and answerable grows in your son's mind when he suffers from consequences of not taking something seriously, beginning with the small issues.

Do You Judge Yourself Because of Mixed Feelings?

Everyone hates mixed feelings. We want to feel good about things all the time, and we will try all sorts of maneuvers to make ourselves feel good about ourselves no matter how bad our people problems become. That's normal, and we all do it. As adults, most of us have developed strategies to assuage our fears and anxieties by talking to ourselves, seeking input from wise people, and generally finding solace wherever it can be had.

Enter teenagers. We don't have many pure feelings about ourselves after the onset of our kids' adolescence. What do teenage men do more naturally than spawn mongrel feelings in parents? Somehow they are able to create discomforts in us. They create anxiety that just won't respond to the type of solutions that work with the other anxieties in your life. And they're pretty subtle in how they plant those mixed feelings in us—second-guessing our decisions, using pregnant pauses in conversation, telling lies, or whispering words under their breath.

Mixed feelings bleed our confidence. They befuddle us, leaving us feeling stuck in an emotional lurch, eroding our hope.

But it doesn't have to be that way. First, you don't need purity in your feelings and self-analysis to be effective as a parent. Although you may feel confused emotionally about what your son is up to, your decision-making processes can operate just fine. Your mental faculties are still operational.

Second, remember that your son's words and actions can swing wildly during this time. He may not even remember today the words he said yesterday that hurt you. If you hold on to his confusing signals, you'll mix yourself up at your own cost. You are the adult here. Let some things slide off your feathers.

Third, sometimes they're right. At times, you will be mixed up and confused because—surprise!—you're not perfect. You may be acting like a jerk and deserve an unpleasant comment or an under-the-breath sneer. But don't let that destroy you. If you demand perfection from yourself, you can expect to get shattered like a crystal goblet dropped on concrete. You're human. You make mistakes. Don't let it steal your confidence.

Have You Succumbed to a Diagnosis?

Sometimes we make ordinary problems of living into diseases. We loosely define a problem, give it a number, and then hang a label on it. We do this too easily for our own good. We, of course, follow this up with tests, medicine, books, therapy, and support groups.

What's the problem with this? It often makes us feel like helpless victims in need of professional care when what we really need is common sense and action. Here are some self-diagnoses that leave some parents bedridden:

- "I have a terrible temper."
- "His father has a drinking problem."
- "I have a divorce in my past."
- "I'm too soft-hearted to make discipline stick."
- "My son and I just see things differently. Our personalities couldn't be more different."

Hiding behind a diagnosis—even one that tells a difficult truth—erodes our confidence. We use a tidy rationale as an excuse for ineffectiveness…and wonder why we're too weak to get out of bed!

Let me encourage you: *You are completely competent to handle 99 percent of all your teenager's behavior.* You are expert enough to handle anything your son throws at you (see chapter 8 for crisis management).

Your *confidence* level will go up as you employ your common sense regularly and use it to build your *competence* one block at a time.

Any young man these days can try to turn the tables and make you, someone else, or some circumstance responsible for problems of his own making. I promise you he has the lingo to pull it off. But if you want your son to learn to be responsible for his own messes, don't let him get away with claiming that your family's got some official disease or disability.

Are You Arguing Your Strength Away?

Don't get hooked into thinking there must be clear, logical reasons for the messes your son makes. Many of the trials and explosions I overhear in supermarket lines and on street corners or read in Ann Landers are complicated by parents trying to plumb the logic their kid used to create the mess in the first place. Trying to figure out the logic of something that has no inherent logic will only erode your confidence.

Our teenagers may not use any logic we'd recognize to get into or out of trouble. They use other tools like excuses, blame shifting, and creative truth twisting. That's why arguing is usually such a waste of time.

Arguments only get somewhere if both parties share some simple assumptions—such as an openness to truth and logic, to listening and learning, and to conceding and changing if necessary. Without ground rules, you're wasting time and energy. But even more important, you're depleting the authority and confidence you need to discipline effectively.

So why do we argue? It's a touching-the-core issue again. We believe that words will change thoughts, hearts, and behavior. We believe that if we win a war of the tongues, we'll affect the core. Perhaps we hope that some priceless nugget will stick.

What's called for is the provocative approach: Don't get a bigger hammer; get a better idea.

House Rules

You can't do police work without a law. I suggest you write and post a manifesto, a list of basic expectations you, as a parent, have the right to enforce. Have it signed and dated by all members of your home. There are many potential rules, just as there are many different kinds of family arrangements to which they apply. But not everything is up for debate. Some things should be cast in stone.

Write them down. You may have to write them as unilateral declarations: *You will always... You will never...*

You know the stance and tone that will work best for your son. But—remembering the goals of discipline—the best commandments are ones that your son owns and cherishes and believes in, even if he doesn't always like them.

The following family agreements are expressed more as statements of identity or personal pride than as dos and don'ts:

A Teenager's Ten Agreements

1. Dad and Mom run the show here. It's not a democracy. My vote counts (a lot), but Dad and Mom decide.
2. I agree to keep Mom and Dad notified of where I am at all times and to ask in advance if permission is necessary.
3. I agree to treat every member of my family, youngest to oldest, with the respect, manners, and thoughtfulness reserved for my most important company.
4. Physical or verbal violence are not OK here—no roughness or out-of-control behavior, no swearing or obscene language, name-calling, or rudeness.
5. Alcohol, drugs, or cigarettes are not allowed in this house or on the property.

6. Sexual intercourse between unmarried persons is not allowed here. Pornography in any form is not allowed in the house.
7. I agree to keep the following schedule: get home by ___ week-nights, ___weekends; bed by _____ on school nights. Sneaking out is not OK.
8. I agree to tell the truth.
9. I agree to respect the property and privacy of others (asking before borrowing, knocking before entering).
10. I agree that important things come first here: Homework comes before television or computer time; chores come before play; church involvement comes first on Sunday.

Make up the rules that best fit your family and post them anywhere you like. Will the rules be followed all the time? Of course not. But with them posted, we now have tremendous leverage to go back and review and take corrective action. You are implementing your system—instead of letting your son's or someone else's system or happenstance rule the day. And you are keeping your confidence level high.

Two Kinds of Discipline

Discipline falls into two broad categories; discipline to address every-day garden-variety troubles and discipline to curb willful defiance.

Keep one thing in mind about teenage boys as we proceed: *Though they are terribly disorganized internally, they aren't stupid.* They might make irresponsible errors and poor choices, but they always do them for reasons—bad reasons quite often, but their own reasons nonetheless.

For example, your son comes up missing after an away basketball game only to show up two hours late with the parents of a pal. Here's his explanation: "I didn't call you because I was with Justin's parents, and I knew you trusted them."

Or how about this one: After an easily avoided fender bender, your son says, "I turned into the traffic lane because I had the right of way and the other driver was being a jerk"?

You're dealing with an inexperienced decision maker trying to get his own way, pondering his options as carefully as an inexperienced brain can.

Everyday rebellion is comprised of the day-in, day-out power play, neglected responsibility, sassy talk, and so on that decorate all our teenagers' days. The motivation for most of these minirevolts is just to get some separation from you. It's normal to experience a constant stream of nicking-and-scraping rebellion, none of which is very remarkable but all of which adds up to normal chaos and stress in life.

Then, of course, there are the outright acts of disobedience and mayhem. The motivation for this kind of rebellion is willful defiance. I once heard that 10 to 20 percent of all kids are born thumbing their noses at the world. Some teens live to defy. Handling this requires some special talents, most of which you didn't learn in school. Let's deal with these in order.

Garden-Variety Disobedience

I believe Christ wants us to be kind to a fault with our teenagers. In Matthew 18, Jesus taught a spine-tingling lesson through a parable. In that story a servant is released from a heavy debt due to the kindness of his master. Then, as the pardoned servant is leaving, he spies a man on the street who owes him a small amount of money. In a fit of anger, he orders the man to pay up or go to jail. Hearing what's transpired, the master orders that the ungrateful servant's debt be reinstated and that he be jailed.

As Christians, we are pardoned by the sacrifice of Christ. Yet we often neglect to extend the same grace to others. We love the sacrifice but forget the mercy business. We forget how indebted we are and fail to pass it on.

Teenagers give us the chance to practice kindness. Believe it or not, unless your son is in jail, your discipline efforts have been somewhat effective up to now—bucking and snorting notwithstanding. Continue to be judicious and tough, but avoid meanness.

The reason we sometimes get mean in our discipline is because we let things build up. We try to be nice and overlook smaller things. We frequently let the sun set on our slowly, steadily fuming hearts. And the fury builds. Anger, as James 1:20 says, never accomplishes the purposes of God. Avoid explosions. It's the right thing to do.

Clarity Is King

To play the discipline game so everybody wins—you stay kind, and he responds to it—follow one single rule: *Make your expectations clear, and make the consequences concrete.* Whatever you do, don't violate this law. Nothing chars you slower or deeper than vague violations of unspecified rules and unclear expectations. Not only are you driven crazy by the offense, but you don't know exactly why. That's bad.

Most problems parents have in controlling the behavior of their teens comes from lack of clarity. Kids don't know specifically what they're to do and not do, and parents haven't clearly enunciated what will happen if the line is breached. Always keep in mind that what's clear to you may be clear in a totally different way to your son.

For example, you say, "Take out the trash, Noah." Since tomorrow is pickup day, this clearly means empty all the baskets into the trash can and take the trash can to the street.

But to Noah, "take out the trash" clearly means emptying any basket he notices that's full and leaving the trash can in the garage for now.

After all, he doesn't have his shoes on, and he'll probably remember to take it to the street in the morning on his way to catch the school bus.

Do yourselves both a favor. Spell out what you want with simple, crystal clarity.

Handle challenges to your clear expectations quickly. Make decisions on matters as fast as you can. Don't hesitate to issue consequences if you said that's what you'd do. The key is to act swiftly and surely.

Sometimes the smallest problems—back talk, procrastination, laziness—build up like barnacles on a ship. The majority of the discipline problems you'll face are just like these tiny barnacles. Don't get lulled into thinking it's all right to put off handling them. Instead, address them with robotic precision, then get on with life. Even behavior in the most chaotic homes can be aired out effectively if you take quicker initiative. Do it before your ship sinks into full-scale meanness.

Establish some simple boundaries. Make a clear list of rules and consequences, then talk about them. Make certain you let your son experience both the joy of following the rules and the blunt-force pounding when they are disregarded.

Let experience do the teaching. It sounds like a no-brainer, but this simple idea works best. Wise parents reward their kids for following the rules. Wise parents don't shield their sons from the full and furious pounding of consequences. But unwise parents violate this elemental law, inadvertently teaching their sons that boundaries—and self-discipline—are no big deal.

Now and then you are going to have to discipline for matters outside your written-in-stone list. Feel free to add to your list any violation that pops up, spell out the consequence as thoughtfully as you can, discuss it, write it down, and enforce it that way forever more. Though the aggravation and time consumption of having to handle these surprises might annoy you, this is the path of least hassle and highest effectiveness.

Willful defiance deserves a willful reply. That's where many of us need the most direction.

As a rule, it works best to use the least amount of force necessary to create behavior change. Warn your son that you are trying to use the easiest weapons first, but you're perfectly willing to pull out the big guns unless there's an immediate change. Nothing works all the time. Sometimes heavier artillery *is* needed.

Managing Industrial-Strength Mayhem

When you have to handle the real tough issues, you need a rip-cord procedure. Certain control situations call for it: unyielding resistance; outright, blatant defiance; dangerous behavior.

Many of the severe discipline tests we face come streaking out of the blue. There's little or no precedent, and frankly, we don't know what to do. The best response allows you to be nice and really tough at the same time. The rule of disengagement works between nations, and it can work for families. It is profoundly simple.

Disengagement allows you to literally "disengage" from all the pressure of disciplining situations. Memorize four simple words: "You'll wish you had/hadn't."

Rather than fight your teenage boy in a discipline situation, simply tell him what you want in a calm, disinterested voice. If he refuses to do as you ask, don't scream or yell, pound or screech, steam or boil. Simply say, "You can do that if you want to, but *you'll wish you hadn't.*" Then go about your business.

As parents, we often forget how much power we have. Think about it. We pay for, initiate, and control everything—transportation, shelter, food, clothing, supplies, luxuries, insurance, vacations, entertainment, education, athletic involvement, just to name a few. It is by virtue of our hard work and dollars that these things appear.

The discipline of disengagement means that rather than tussle and scrap, you simply inform him that negative consequences will happen soon enough—and walk away. This approach allows you to handle big problems in a low-anxiety, clearheaded, fair manner.

You'll have to learn to do this. Boiling internally and forcing compliance comes too naturally for many of us. Soon, perhaps within hours or days, he'll need something only you can provide—which is, as you just saw, virtually everything. Then, slightly stiffening your backbone, remind him that you warned him that he'd be sorry, and the time is now.

And don't back down.

Jake and the Beanstalk

Here's a simple illustration of how this worked in real life. Once my son Jake just flat-out refused to do his lawn-mowing chores. It was an "out of the blue" moment. Rather than fight, I chose to disengage; I said, "You can refuse to do this, Jake, but you'll wish you hadn't."

I did the lawn without complaint or excess stomach acid.

Two days later came the educational part. He had a need that only I could fill: He'd made plans with his friends to hit golf balls at the range, and he needed a ride. I simply reminded him that I had said he would wish he had mowed the lawn, and now was the time. I didn't take him. In a sudden, very simple and awful moment for him, my credibility grew like a beanstalk, as did his understanding of how life *really* works.

I didn't force change; I provoked it.

Two things empower this approach. First, the onus of change is completely *on him*. You don't need to challenge and bluff, because the problem—and the consequences (whatever you decide them to be)—are entirely his problem. There's no more need to threaten or blow up.

Second, you have the opportunity to increase your own personal credibility and value. Taking things—like you—for granted starts early in your son's life. To be really healthy, he needs occasional reminders that his life could be much worse were it not for your kindness and hard work. Teenagers are a self-absorbed lot at times, so subtle wake-up shakes are good.

During high-temperature moments, this also helps you avoid making outbursts and threats that you'll later feel idiotic about, back off on, or forget:

- *"You're grounded until you're sixty-five!"*
- *"You're a complete disappointment as a son!"*

Attacks blurted out in anger only harm, and threats are meaningless. Your credibility grows when you follow through on your threats. No lectures, just gritty experience.

You may find it useful to write down where and when disengagements have occurred in your home. Once it had been weeks before I found a slip of paper with an incident marked on it that I decided to act on. Calling in a weeks-old "deal" may sound harsh, and it is. But it reflects adult realities—taxes, loans, and contracts don't get less binding with time. And I've only had to do it one or two times. My kids have learned I'm for real. I urge you to be for real too.

Parental Accidents

Despite your valiant attempts to avoid it, you're going to blow up and make mistakes. What should you do about accidents that evolve into shouting matches, harsh words, hurt feelings, and maybe physical violence?

Keep an eye on yourself. Be as deliberate as possible, pausing frequently in heated conversations to verify what you want to accomplish. Then measure your words carefully and speak with precision about problems you're having:

- "Kyle, I'm trying very hard to maintain my composure with you, and I don't want to blow up."
- "I sometimes get ahead of myself and lose control, Andy. Help me here."
- "My brain gets pretty scrambled when we talk like this, Pete."

This kind of self-monitoring is tough in the midst of an explosion. But you can rein yourself in faster than you can rein him in, so control what you can as quickly as you can.

It's fine to ask for a time-out to think things over. If a conversation goes haywire, ask for five, ten, or twenty minutes to cool down and think. You can reconvene when things mellow a bit and everyone is thinking clearer. Encourage him to use time-outs as well if he needs one.

A Closer Focus

Strategic Planning

The next time a confrontation or difficult encounter occurs between you and your son, take a moment and ask yourself, *What can I do differently?* It won't be easy. The hardest part is that you're in a rut and you handle most unusual situations in the same usual way every time. Write down your different plan (or a range of options) for next time.

Reach for What Holds You Together

In high-pressure moments we tend to forget that the deep ties that bind us are much stronger than the temporal forces dividing us. Remember those things that bind you and your son together:

- love
- good memories
- family history
- promises
- shared understandings and secrets
- shared likes or dislikes
- identity
- your history of survival together
- your cooking

When your words threaten to go up in heat and smoke, reach for a different set of truths. Talk from the perspective of the unchangeable things that hold your lives tightly together:

- "Derek, I'm your biggest fan in the whole world."
- "Jed, I know you care a lot about other people's feelings and you didn't expect things to work out this way."
- "Look, I'm absolutely sure we're going to work this through, even though we're really upset right now."

When you do this, you are stepping outside of a situation that may have become stalemated or anguished to remind him and yourself of the bigger picture. And the bigger picture is all good. Instead of reaching for a bigger hammer, you're reaching for a better idea. And you're taking charge in a most surprising and redemptive way.

Eat Crow

Always reserve the right to say, "I was wrong. I'm sorry. Will you forgive me?" These are hard words. Power words. And they may not always be accepted immediately, especially if you've dealt a biting word or a physical blow. But a meal of crow has always been a key ingredient in the menu of healthy parents. Just remember that, in general, the harder it is to say something, the more it probably needs being said. Admitting you've been wrong *and meaning it* is salve.

Does the young man in front of you deserve an apology for your errors and misbehaviors any less than your spouse, your neighbor, or your boss would?

Admission and apology words will connect deeply with your son. They speak to his real desire to have a close relationship with you. He wants to believe good things about you. He wants to know that his opinions matter to you, that his brain works well enough to gain your respect.

Maybe all you have to do to succeed in discipline is say you're sorry.

A Brief Debrief

Since discipline is about training, a commitment to rigorous evaluation as you go along makes a lot of sense. I recommend that you debrief yourself after every negative encounter. You don't need to fume, squirm, pout, worry, and anguish. Instead, ask yourself these simple questions:

- What did I want to happen?
- What did I get?
- What broke down?
- What could I have done better?
- What can I do differently now?

If you have the time, consider starting a journal and adding your culled insight. Spend your energy more fully exploring and collecting new insights rather than grinding your teeth and burning your stomach lining. Write out on paper the answers to these questions. If you must, ask for others' input—or talk to the dog as a last resort. But don't stop until you've done a thorough job of answering the questions.

Especially the last one. Not long ago I had a raging problem with a teenager in my life. He had failed me badly. It cost me some money, and I was hot. I fumed for days. I needed to do that before I opened my mouth to him. After several days and a cooler head, the question that finally came to me and changed everything was: *What can I do differently?*

It's the kind of provocative question a parent can miss in the midst of all those daily "training opportunities."

Chapter Seven

Conflict of Interests

Coping strategies for little arguments and big rebellions

Parents of teens may find themselves wondering if they'll ever experience family peace again. Some days we'd settle for any old ceasefire. Then just about the time we get one teenager to the negotiating table, the next younger child fires off a volley of his own.

This chapter is for parents who find themselves in warlike power struggles. Of course, what's happening is *not* war. In your deepest hearts, both you and your son want a *win-win* situation. Parenting a teen is more like a long, drawn-out court case where the prosecution and defense keep switching sides—and the jury is always deadlocked. The court proceedings can range from the least significant matters (Who made what passing remark and how?) to some major head butting (Will he or won't he give a rip about school?).

Maybe you can relate.

We'd all love to have cooperative and enthusiastic adolescents all the time. Teens are only occasionally like that. More often they're varying shades of difficult. Many teenagers feel like the world is out to corner them, to rob them of their precious liberty. The handiest way to vent their paranoia is to take it out on you, either by ignoring you or arguing with you about every little thing.

Remember fighting with your own parents? They seemed so out of it. My father was a college professor. He wore his hair longer, invited Black Panthers and hippies to dinner, and occasionally shocked us with hip college lingo. But do you think I was impressed? He could've been the coolest guy in the world, and we kids still would've thought he was an old-timer! I remember thinking, *Man, this guy just doesn't get it!*

Typical teen opposition is a power contest you're just not supposed to win, at least not by ordinary rules. But we can win—and so can our kids—if we understand what's really happening and how to turn normal family conflicts into the nurturing ground for man-making.

Points of Rebellion

You might wonder why, if you're following the rules of good, basic discipline, you still have conflicts. Raising young men is not neat or clean. Exceptions seem the rule, circumstances keep on extenuating, and intentions and actual performance have a way of rarely coinciding.

For example, every parenting decision seems to set up another one. Your son is out with friends three hours past his curfew. Do you prosecute and go for the grounding without parole? If your son is grounded for a week without friends, can he play basketball outside with his brother and his brother's friend?

This environment makes for turmoil. Most arguments start when conflicts occur in two major categories:

- You don't like something he did and ask for an accounting.
- You respond to what he did with discipline, and he doesn't like it.

Let's look at typical teen responses in each of these scenarios. First, let's say you don't like something he did, and his response is to…

Make excuses. These usually start with, "I didn't mean to," or "I didn't know," or "But I…" (for example, "I didn't mean to stay out till 2 A.M. There was no clock!").

Shift the blame. Your son blames someone else. "I told John that I needed to get home, but he told this girl that he'd take her home first, and…"

Tell conflicting stories. "But that's not what happened," or "Sam's mom is lying!"

Claim he didn't understand. "I had no idea that when you said I couldn't go to that party with Jeff that you'd mind if I went with Steve. I thought you just didn't want me hanging out with Jeff. He wasn't there!"

Next, let's consider the second situation. He doesn't like how you responded to what he did (he objects to the punishment), and his argument is based on…

Another misunderstanding. "When you said I'd be grounded, it didn't include football practice! I would have made sure I was home on time if I'd known that."

The fact of his remorse. "But I'm sorry! I won't do it again. I know you're serious! You don't need to punish me. I've learned my lesson already. Really."

Threats against the effectiveness of your plan. He might actually try to talk you out of punishing him on the basis that he's decided it won't work. "If you take my car away, I'll just borrow Mike's extra car anyway!" Or, "If you ground me for sassing you, it's not going to make me talk any nicer."

You're cruel and unfair. "When Mary [the little sister] slammed her door last week, she didn't have to do extra chores." Or, "A week of grounding is way too long for anybody! No one else I know would ever get in that much trouble just for swearing."

Where's Johnny Cochran when you need him?

Choosing Your Response

Before your get tangled up in a verbal wrangling match, ask yourself two important questions:

1. Does my son's complaint warrant discussion—or is he simply playing with a loophole in my system?

2. Are we both emotionally ready to come to the table—or should we recess?

Sometimes you'll need to talk through every detail and feeling and then review your rulings and decisions, but there's no need for this if what you're getting is simply the standard young male urge to resist. Young men routinely resist a lot of things—pain, work, a new advance in responsibility, vegetables. A parent's job is to live with that resistance. However, if talk can help, you may have an opportunity for a successful argument (see the next section). Sometimes the issue is not the

---

A Closer Focus

Quiet Storms

Some guys are what I would call "quiet storms." They have a low-level, intense anger that never really flares but is always threatening. Perhaps their anger gets funneled into critical attitudes, negative comments, chronic failure, or depression. These kids deserve the same kind of serious, problem-solving attention as the flamethrowers.

Does your son need a closer relationship with a positive male? Do what you can to create that proximity (to a church youth group leader, a martial-arts instructor, a coach, or a tutor).

content of the decision but the state of the adversaries. If you feel like you're in a war zone, you probably are. A recess is the right choice. The following can help you measure where you are on this general progression. It's simple to use. Generally, do not attempt a discussion if either of you is exhibiting behavior above the line of this chart. Attempting a dialogue anywhere near the middle will be frustrating but might be worth a try—you be the judge. Don't be afraid to recess if the situation escalates over the line. We'll look more at "recessing" in a minute.

Low Chance for Quick Resolution (take a recess)
violence
slamming doors or hitting objects
swearing/yelling
lying, threatening
heated or irrational accusations
name-calling
withdrawing (leaving room as a gesture)
pouting

---

blaming, being a victim
holding on to "always" or "never"
rationalizing
arguing feelings: "You make me mad."
discussing the issues: "When you do this . . ."
openness to listening and self-assessment
asking questions; willing to reconsider or change
accepting responsibility
relaxed feedback of other person's point of view
High Chance of Quick Resolution (choose to engage)

How to Have a Successful Argument

Have you ever comfortably disagreed with someone then effectively arrived at a decision agreeable to you both? Successful disagreement occurs when defenses are kept in check and when each party makes a conscious decision to be more united than divided. These objectives can be met with your son. Here's how.

Establish common ground. In Proverbs 20:5, Solomon said that wisdom resides in all of us and the wise person will draw it out of another. Unity is something everyone in a family shares, and we know it. But relations between family members often sour because we forget about or downplay the significance of what we hold in common. Recovering that view requires that everyone step back and assess what we share in common before proceeding too far down the path of disagreement.

How do you do that with a teenage boy? Psychologists use a trick they call "utilization." I call it the "1 percent overlap" rule. The 1 percent overlap rule says that you can turn a bad "people situation" into a good one by finding the 1 percent where you agree.

It might look like this: Your son wants to smoke cigars. Cigars won't kill him. Cigars won't ruin his genes. Cigars will harm his lungs, depending on how many, how often, and to what degree he smokes them. Cigars will make his breath stink. Cigars will make people think he's a Republican. All these things your son claims he can live with.

You still don't want him smoking cigars.

What might be the 1 percent overlap here? If it were my son, the 1 percent overlap (what we both absolutely agree on) is that we care about his life. "Cigars really aren't good for anyone's health." Since we both want to protect his life, we'll have a successful conversation on this topic if we base our comments and discussion on that point of overlap rather than on countless others that lead to hostility.

Will it be 100 percent smooth? No way!

Will it always work? Nothing "always" works.

Will it help? Try it and see.

Stick to the facts. Keep to the facts as much as you can, and remind your son to do the same. Offer to police each other on this. It might sound like this:

- "Look, you don't know what I was feeling or thinking unless I tell you."
- "OK, we both know you backed into the telephone pole. I want to try to figure out why it happened without getting so upset about what it's going to cost. Let me take a deep breath…"

You don't want to intentionally insult your son or assault his integrity. Make sure he knows it. He might like to hear that you aren't out to

---

A Closer Focus

Caught in the Back Talk

Boys like to tease, challenge, and verbally joust. Teenage boys smart off because (1) they feel relaxed with you, (2) they're trying to best you in some way, or (3) they're upset with you. Let the relaxed stuff go. "Boy banter" shouldn't be misinterpreted for lack of respect. Banter back if you like.

But, if you're hearing razor-edged comments, try to understand the source of frustration. What's vital is to have a family mechanism in place to be candid without being mean. Make the mechanism a simple statement: "You sound mad." Keep alluding to what you hear that's not being said. That will reveal the deeper frustration, which can then be addressed or repaired.

destroy his life (which a large number of teenagers actually believe). If at any time during a disagreement you feel your intentions are misunderstood, go back and reiterate them:

- "You're a great guy, and you try hard. That doesn't change just 'cause I'm really mad at you right now. We just have to figure out how to keep this from happening again."

Don't escalate. Most people become increasingly defensive in the midst of tension and disagreement (especially if the problem has been postponed or has simmered for a long time). Teenagers sometimes say things that feel like a verbal shove. These words "polarize" us, push us into a corner, and make us want to push back using polarizing words of our own, such as, "We'll see about that!" or "I've had just about enough!" or "You'll wish you'd never been born." Threats, challenges, even denying that there's a problem all fall into the category of "polarizing." These moves only make things worse.

We escalate a conflict automatically when we:

- increase our volume
- raise the stakes of the outcome
- bring up old, hurtful business
- step on personal vulnerabilities
- insist on black-and-white thinking (He's all wrong, you're all right; he's a complete fool, you're a flawless, victimized dad.)
- assume the worst—about motives or the possibility of change
- use rudeness or violence to provoke a response
- persist in fighting when white flags (sincere listening, apologies, concessions) are showing

James said, "The anger of man does not achieve the righteousness of God" (James 1:20, NASB). He must've been through some angry, polarized moments himself and seen them for the dead ends they are. A parent always loses when he or she stoops to pushing back or turning up the heat needlessly.

Take turns. Interpret what you hear each other saying:

- "You tried to call home but no one answered, so you felt you had no choice but to…"

Be careful about tone of voice here. There's a world of difference in the following rendition:

- "OK (you roll your eyes here, and your voice rises until it's a falsetto by the end of the sentence), so you're saying that even though you're a straight-A student it never occurred to you to…?"

If either interpretation is wrong, ask for clarification or offer it as needed. Each person must be satisfied that the other party knows and thoroughly understands the position of the other before you can successfully proceed. Take as much time as necessary to do this.

Your teenager will be much more likely to discuss things openly if he trusts that you're not going to bash him in the head or rob him of his freedom in a one-sided bloodbath. As an investment in your young man, treat him like one, even if he's letting you down at the moment. Agree on give-and-take, be silent when the other person is speaking, and reject power or escalation moves. Good things will happen.

Be deliberate. You have many options available to you during arguments, and you'll do yourself a favor by opening your mind to as many as possible. For example, you don't have to immediately answer every question posed by your teenager. You don't need to answer questions you're not prepared to answer.

Jesus gave us an illustration of this. In John 8, a woman caught in the act of adultery was brought to Jesus. The temple officials were indignant at Jesus and wanted to entrap Him. They thought they had set the perfect religious snare and were eager to see what Jesus would say.

As usual, He surprised them all. He said nothing. As they harangued Him, Jesus chose to bend over and write in the dirt. After He'd written for a while He stood and said, in effect, "Go ahead. Kill her. Let the one of you who has no sin cast the first stone." Then He bent over and wrote some more. When He stood again, nobody was there except the woman. "Go and sin no more," He said. His careful delay added greatly to the effect of what He wanted to demonstrate.

No matter what the pressure of the moment might be, you have every right to say, "I don't know how I feel about that yet" or, "I need to make a decision; I'll let you know." Exercise self-control and reasoning, and answer only when you are able to say what you mean.

A Closer Focus

Setting Ground Rules

Over popcorn, ask the family to come up with your own fair-fight rules. Ask: What makes a fight fair anyway? How can we complain so something good happens? What are our rules about physical abuse against people or property? Some hot topics you could discuss include screaming, rolling one's eyes in disgust, sarcasm, walking away, bringing up past problems just to hurt the other person, name-calling, interruptions, and listening. Post your family's personal fair-fight rules and put them to work.

Case closed (for now). You'll reach a point (usually before your son does) when you know there's no purpose in continuing the argument. You need to take a recess when:

- You're deadlocked.
- You're exhausted.
- You've been clear, and you've heard your son out; all that's left now is the need for your son to accept your rules.
- You need more time to think through the issues or gather facts.

In most cases, when you call a recess you should set a time when you will talk again. That gives you implied control over the situation. You might also want to give each party some sort of assignment to carry out in the meantime. Agreeing on anything, even a new meeting time, may be your first step toward common ground and success. And it shows that you care enough not to ignore a difficulty in your relationship with your son.

Conflict Comes with a Promise

Healthy conflict takes the normal tensions and disagreements of the teen years and turns them into the stuff of greatness—the ability to talk about feelings, responsibility, respect, and sensitivity toward others, a willingness to work through disagreements.

All this conflict stuff reminds me of some wisdom from the great actor Peter Ustinov: "Parents are the bones on which children sharpen their teeth." That *is* how it feels, isn't it! But at least our lives have added up to something eternally useful.

You might feel mercilessly gnawed upon now, but if you seize the opportunity in conflict, a boss down the road is going to give your son a promotion (because he can be a team player in high-pressure situations). A daughter-in-law in years to come is going to thank you for giving her a wonderful husband (because he knows how to listen, express himself, and resolve hard feelings appropriately).

Try another metaphor: Imagine that you are the curb, and your son is the driver of his life. Bumping the curb is part of learning. If he never hits the curb, you can be sure he either never left the garage, doesn't feel safe enough to test the boundaries, or is going to really slam hard later on.

The time will come all too quickly when conflict with your son will fade. Most of your life will be different—more focused on friendship, encouragement, sharing. What's going on now is a short and intense season when you have an opportunity to establish some habits in your young man that will last a lifetime.

That opportunity comes wrapped in conflict more often than we'd like. But the future holds more harmony than hate for you both. Count on it. Pray for it. Expect it.

Chapter Eight

911—Help!

Changing the course of a teen in deep trouble

An old friend of mine recently shared some bad news. This father is very proud and strong, and his son is hardheaded and extremely immature. One night the muleheaded kid borrowed his dad's car, got drunk, and smashed up himself and two buddies. His parents received the dreaded call from the hospital and rushed to his side. Their son recovered perfectly, but his buddies were more seriously injured, creating long and bitter litigation, family fractures, and long-term troubles that continue to this day.

My friend, the boy's father, confessed to me that he'd shielded his son's drinking habit from everyone. Had it not been for the accident, the problem might never have come to light. But my friend's steadfast denial and silence only worsened the problem.

Most of us have difficulty admitting when our kids are in serious trouble. But sometimes we find ourselves with no other choice. Things get out of control. Someone else has to come to the rescue.

Nearly everything in this book assumes you'll get the ordinary list of trouble that comes with kids like fleas come with dogs. This chapter, however, reaches a little further. We all need to be prepared for the serious problems that might come our way.

Let's get ready.

Careening Out of Control

A legitimate parenting crisis occurs when you have to handle something damaging, frightening, or illegal that your son has done—something that seems beyond your ability to manage.

- Your son refuses to obey rules or adhere to punishments.
- Your son is involved in drugs and drinking.
- Your son is choosing all the wrong friends.
- Your son is dangerously angry, depressed, or suicidal.
- Your son commits crimes.
- Your son is being sexually foolish.
- Your son has a violent temper and gets physical.
- Your son is risking his life or health or future.

A crisis has a way of paralyzing even the most resourceful mom or dad. We seem to be stuck in our worst nightmare. And behind all the emotional trauma, stress, and danger lurks what we fear most—the threat that our kid's life won't turn out; that all our love and affection will somehow be wasted.

We're terrified that the pain of the moment will turn into lifelong negative consequences and patterns. We desperately need to keep perspective, to hang on to hope, and to figure out what to do next.

If you're the parent of a teenage son in crisis, you *do* have reasons for optimism. Besides your strong faith in God, you've had a lot of practice with your son by this point. And since you've been tested personally many times, those lessons and experiences have filled your medic bags with tools sufficient to properly treat most troubles. But the very nature of a crisis means you don't have everything you need. Your ability to control your son seems suddenly and mysteriously absent.

Oxygen, Please!

Let me help you think through some key issues, learn to assess situations, and identify resources for further help. The first person I want to deal with in this crisis is you—the parent. You need to keep breathing! You'll know you're ready to handle your son's situation when you have your own emotional reactions in check enough to move from what happened to active problem solving.

Don't scold yourself if your initial reactions are bad. Just handle those first moments or hours the best you can, then settle down to think and consider options.

Work the "now" problem first. When a crisis hits, your first instinct might lead you to see nothing but disaster and hopelessness in the future and remorse in the past. Instead, keep your eyes focused on the immediate problem and deal with each one in order. If you try to handle too many problems at once, you'll panic.

Just look at one at time, and don't fix number nine on the list until you've dealt with one, two, three, and so on.

Find a rescuer. Parenting teens is mostly about knowing how to influence without controlling, but in a crisis, someone has to seize firm control. A rescuer is a person or agency that will help you regain control. You need one now.

Rescuers know how to work the system (school systems, financial systems, legal systems, family systems) to help you fix the "now" problems. They might be attorneys, friends, clergy, paramedics, or your son's peers.

Their role is to provide objective but caring counsel when you may not be thinking straight. At this point, what you need is intervention, not long-term care. Later you'll be ready to tackle some of the underlying problems and root causes.

Recruit a long-term helper. A long-term helper will assist you in addressing the deeper problem. This helper can be a professional counselor, a family therapist, a clergyperson, a high-impact youth worker, a mentor, or a sharp peer. Any long-term helper you choose should be able to communicate certain important messages to your son about what all this help means:

- Your son is responsible for his own actions and his own future.
- You, the parent, are not Santa Claus and won't always show up if he refuses to change.
- Growing up is about growing up—it's hard, it's the real thing, and it's something only he can do for himself (but he doesn't have to do his growing up alone).

Remember when you start searching for a counselor, pastor, psychologist, or psychiatrist that professional credentials don't necessarily mean a person is blessed with real life-changing skills. I always recommend rigorous comparison shopping and prayerful choices.

A Crisis Insurance Policy

Sometimes, despite your best efforts, your son won't shift course. He seems bent on traveling the hard road. Memorize these three questions to ask your son. They will act as an insurance policy with cash value during those tough tests still ahead. They will also help you get at deeper issues of conduct (and give you something sensible and relaxed to think about until you can think up something better).

1. "Do you want to fix this?" I started asking teenagers this question several years ago out of professional frustration. It seemed to me that the real agenda of many teenagers in my counseling practice was to complain. Having spent fruitless hours counseling them only to hear it all rejected, it seemed a fair question.

This question establishes both an expectation and a mood of sincere curiosity and helpfulness. If he says yes, then begins shooting down all your advice and ideas, ask the question again: "Do you really want to fix this problem?" If he answers no, either explore the consequences of failing to fix it or walk away and spend your time elsewhere until he's stewed some more.

2. "What do you want from me?" I've used this million-dollar question countless times with chronic bad boys for one simple reason: Boys in trouble are used to getting lectures. They're accustomed to people trying to force goodness into them. They're not used to people in authority simply asking what it is they want from the helper.

Maybe you can hear your son answering, "I don't want anything from you." In my experience, a kid in crisis usually won't say that. Only kids who feel the crisis is past or that they're untouchable will say that—and stand by it over and over again. Those kids are deluding themselves and need professional help if they persist.

Try asking your son this question and notice the amount of freedom it provides you. It's a great conversation starter even when everything is fine.

3. "If I do what you want, how do I know you'll change?" This is a fair, adult-to-adult question. Many kids can't answer it, however, because kids causing big problems aren't usually reliable enough to give their word and stand by it. But since you might be the only one willing to help this kid out of the mess, he really hasn't got the luxury of ignoring the question. Stay tough, and don't let him off the hook. Demand an answer.

If he does tell you how you'll know he's changed, ask for specifics and for time frames. If he gets busted stealing sunglasses and he says he'll never do it again because he's learned his lesson, make him get specific. Ask him what lesson, when he learned it, when he can see himself applying it, and what he'll do differently next time. These are fair questions that demand fair answers before you jump to the rescue.

A Laundry List of Last Resorts

"Can I kick him out?" Of course you can. It would be a heartbreaking decision, one not to be taken lightly, but if your son is physically violent, abusing drugs, chronically depressed, delusional, or suicidal, the best place for him may be somewhere that he can get the appropriate help and protection—while you receive the same. The most loving thing you can do for him might be to get him out of your house. That could be to a foster home, a hospital, an uncle in a faraway place, a treatment program, or a military school. It should never be just "out"—to let him stay with his friends or fend for himself.

"Should I leave him in jail?" I've urged many parents to let young Fred chill in jail for a while. Jails are unique institutions of higher learning.

A Closer Focus

Should I Snoop?

No. I don't think it's right or fair to snoop. Certainly there are times when you'll accidentally find a surprise in a pants pocket, or while looking for your sweatshirt in his dresser, you'll find something you wish you hadn't. You can't avoid those unintentional discoveries.

Snooping leaves you feeling cheap, and it leaves your son feeling invaded and betrayed.

They work well with certain types of kids. Chances are extremely high that home and wiser behavior will take on the greatest appeal to a sensible kid. If your son is a repeat offender or if your words and efforts are roundly ignored, let him come to his senses behind bars. You may struggle with two powerful parental instincts during all this: *to protect* and *to do something*. Weather this emotional turmoil—letting him sit in jail is doing both.

"What about a prescription to sedate or otherwise control him?" Using pharmacology to change behavior is scary, and I have lots of reservations about it, but I'm also fascinated. I can tell you more stories of miraculous recoveries involving the intelligent use of medicine than of any form of psychotherapy available today.

If a professional suggests a prescription for your son, I suggest you avoid it as long as you can. Personally, I just don't like the thought of drugging young guys. It's way too easily abused. But if you've come to the end of your rope, don't feel bad about trying medication on a provisional basis. If it brings the results you expect and you like them, so much the better. Be as thorough as possible when questioning doctors about how the drugs work and their side effects. And demand that your son be monitored carefully.

"What if he tries suicide?" Suicide is one of the leading causes of death among teenagers—and it's not just something that happens to other people's kids. Unfortunately, much of today's music and literature have planted a nihilistic, "life-makes-no-sense" mind-set into the heads of many kids who are perfectly fine otherwise. In the end, this "despair" becomes glamorized and romanticized.

If your son tries suicide or threatens it in any way, get help immediately. Always take seriously danger signs such as dramatic shifts in behavior, long withdrawals, a marked loss of appetite, a critical loss in a relationship or other significant involvement, a sudden abandoning of lifelong interests or dreams, or hopeless comments about his life or future. In almost all cases when a teenager threatens suicide, it's a bluff or a call for help, but always treat it like the real thing. Stay in his presence as long as possible. Suicide victims rarely "succeed" in front of an audience. Second, keep him talking. In almost every case of suicide, the person feels alone, helpless, worthless, and empty. Talking with someone who just listens can easily forestall the moment when a suicidal person might be overcome by the sudden urge to act. Third, remember that suicide is usually an impulsive act. Almost never does somebody want to die. What he seeks is relief. Stay with him and keep him talking through the crisis.

Finger Ribbons

When we're going through the inferno, we're focused on just that—*getting through*. During those days and hours, a dad is likely to miss an important meeting and forget to shave. Mom is just as prone to start out for the market in her slippers. Who can remember the details when the walls are crashing down?

But some things are worth remembering, no matter how hot the fire. Consider these pointers as brightly colored ribbons passed along from parents who've been there. If you tie them on as reminders, you *will* get through.

Remember you are only parents. Many great parents are driven to the edge of insanity believing it's their responsibility to totally outfit their teens for life. That belief can be frustrating and exhausting. It's completely unrealistic to take complete responsibility for all your son's choices. Growing up is all about learning autonomy—and that means a lot of messes. Even God had to suffer through it with His children, the Jews (and He was the perfect parent).

Remember there's a limit to the amount of influence you can exert. Unfortunately, it's virtually impossible to know where this limit lies. Therefore it's vital to present yourself in the most attractive and approachable manner possible as often as possible. Will he absorb all you have? Never! Will he appreciate your timely wisdom and concern? Dream on! Comfort yourself by remembering that he has, for the same reason, missed out on some of your unhelpful input too.

Remember that real life is the best teacher. Sometimes you have to prepare yourself to get out of the way and let life take over your son's education. And your teen will crash, burn, cry, and learn, just like you did. And then he'll be smart. Like you. The pattern has been cycling for generations.

A Closer Focus

Pot and Beyond

The reason your son might smoke pot and use harder drugs usually has nothing to do with the reason he will say he uses them. Whereas cigarettes are often tried in a fit of harmless experimentation, pot is a step in the direction of outright rebellion or a call for help. Harder drugs are a full-blown plea.

Brief, general advice doesn't do much good here. You're doing your best when you consult your team of advisers (your circle of friends and confidantes). Focus on finding out what kind of holes he's trying to fill.

If your son is sinking into regular pot use or playing around with any of the more dangerous drugs, you need to act quickly and decisively. Ask your team to help you develop an intervention plan. Now's the time to be audaciously present and to talk openly and persistently with your son.

Expect him at some point to ridicule your reason and laugh off your wisdom. Don't let it get under your skin. It's at that moment that your teen is ready for the best, most effective teacher he'll ever know. Her name is "real life," and she instructs in a school called Hard Knocks High.

This school has some magna cum laude graduates. Maybe you're one. Today you probably believe many of the same things your parents believed. You surely didn't get it from them. In fact, you probably summarily rejected them and their old-fogy wisdom. Then life took over. She's tough. She doesn't budge or bend. Over time, you discovered that some of those lessons weren't so bad.

The single greatest advantage of this method of learning is that it works. A disadvantage is that it usually hurts at the time. Another is that Mom and Dad don't get any credit until much later.

Remember, you're still in control of a lot. When you must converse about difficulties, keep your cool and don't be tricked into power battles. As a parent, you're still in charge of a lot: food, entertainment, travel, phones, housing, and much more. Your teenager has no idea what his life would be like without you. When your son defies you, use your advantages wisely. Remember, you're his genie in the bottle, and he may have forgotten that. Remember disengagement (chapter 6). Remember to be provocatively calm and surprising.

Remember that time passes. Time changes everything, including teens and police records, scrapes at school, legal entanglements, hormone levels, memories… Time is your friend.

"9-1-1, I'm Okay…"

No one fully understands what you're going through when you face huge disappointments and crisis moments. But when God chose you to be

Mom or Dad for your son, He really did know about this challenge. He's not surprised. And He's not for a minute in doubt about this: You're the parent of choice for this test and this young man in the making.

Think about another possibility: Maybe the crisis is for *you.* Maybe *you* are the child whom God the Father is trying to teach something invaluable right now. You wouldn't want to experience all this pain and miss the payoff.

In God's economy, crisis cracks the shell of everyday-ness. Crisis nearly always lets the extraordinary out—of your life and of your son's. With the sledgehammer of consequences, it breaks through limitations and deafness and carelessness. Some hardheaded young men just don't grow up without it—and some of us parents don't either. That's why I encourage you to look for the up side in every crisis you face. Troubles bring candor, new input and perspective, sudden awakenings…

Sometimes what seems to be the worst thing can turn out, in the long run, to be the finest blessing of all.

PART THREE

SHAPING A MAN
READY FOR LIFE

Chapter Nine

Main Attractions

A guy's guide to sexuality, chivalry, and girls

Once when I sat in the home office of a friend, his teenage daughter came into the room with a long face. She'd been on a first date the prior night, and it hadn't gone well. We asked her about it. She hesitated to discuss details, but she recited that familiar lament: "Guys only want one thing!"

My friend never blinked. He looked at her with a kindly smile and said, "You seem surprised."

After she left, my friend turned to me and said, "Boys haven't changed much since I was a kid." As if I needed to be told.

Boys haven't changed much. Books have been devoted to teenage male sexual behavior, and often the assumptions contradict what many of us feel is right and proper. Thankfully, our sexual attitudes appear to be swinging from "anything goes" to sensibility and safety. But the sexual realities that drive teenage boys are undeniable.

That'll never change. Young men are on permanent boil. Hormones drive the deep desire for pleasure. And all we can do is frantically dream up new ways to keep the bubbling under control!

As parents of teenage boys, we fear that our sons will not exercise wisdom in controlling their sexual urges. We worry about pornography, masturbation, premarital sex, sexually transmitted diseases, and unwanted pregnancy. We also care that our sons treat girls with respect. In fact, this is one of the hardest areas to discuss. And since we usually carry around a lot of sexual baggage of our own, we parents have our work cut out for us!

I have a suggestion: Rather than rehash, let's reorient. We usually stop too short when we deal with boys and sexuality. We worry almost exclusively about stopping or controlling the sexual stuff. We talk to our sons about dating limits, purity, and keeping their hands to themselves. But we too often fail to equip our boys with skills to relate to girls as people first. Without meaning to, we plant the assumption and reinforce the idea that a boy's main goal with girls is sex, not friendship and learning.

If we want our teenage boys to respect girls sexually, then we need to teach them how to interact with their minds first.

The Big Celebration (with Flashing Yellow Lights)

Sex is one of God's most wondrous and enjoyable invitations to celebrate—in the proper situation. The proper situation is marriage. Sex under any other circumstances is an open invitation to trouble. Though momentarily exhilarating, sex outside of marriage is a clear and often devastating violation of what works for success in life.

Sexual energy, however, especially in someone as hormonally charged as your teenage son, is a wildly strong and surprising force. It begins in your son's life during these years, peaks at eighteen, and won't burn out for a long, long time. Like everything else in life, proper sexuality requires a degree of self-control and maturity, all of which require time to develop. The intervening years (and it will be years) that pass before sexual judgment and maturity develop are the gauntlet all responsible males must run.

Parents with a Plan

The teenage years are the age of lost innocence. The scales fall from our boy's eyes, and he sees many new things. Some people think this loss of innocence is bad. But we need to view our son's loss of innocence as a good thing and find ways to make it more effective.

Here are three suggestions:

Get informed. Sexuality is complex, medically speaking. If there are aspects of sexuality you don't understand, ask. Read a book, talk to your doctor, phone a hospital, call a radio show—just get the information! Your lack of information could contribute to someone losing his or her life, so study up.

Say "sex." Many of us carry around lots of baggage about sex. For some it's wholesome and delightful. For others it means bad experiences, getting caught in embarrassing situations, broken dreams, diseases, abortions, or sexual defilement at the hands of criminals. The vast majority of us have some sorry or at least awkward tales to tell.

Whatever our experience, we're wise as parents to learn to talk about sex with our children with some degree of candor and comfort. It's one of the most powerful forces on the planet, and it's unwise to deny or ignore it. Sure, you want to protect your son from explicit pictures and movies, but be careful to avoid transmitting a derogatory message in the process of restricting it. Sex is beautiful if handled well.

To believe that sex is great and to communicate it to our sons, we may have to overcome much of our own discomfort. We have to learn to talk.

Confront misinformation quickly. Research shows that most of the information your son has about sex comes from his peers. Yet teens are notoriously ignorant and superstitious about girls in general and sex specifically. They spread misinformation about girls they've known both personally and vicariously and spread fabrications to suit their imaginations. (If you want a list, ask any man.)

Your son is being bombarded almost constantly with slanted and biased information designed to leverage certain dark hopes he has about girls. Most of those perceptions about girls aren't true, much less helpful. Girls are portrayed in advertisements as seductive temptresses with odd tastes in cola, clothes, and cigarettes.

All this input is very compelling in the minds of clueless guys searching for answers. Do your part to confront ignorance. No need for drama or scolding here. Just speak the truth without apology.

A Twisted Image

Not long ago I was at a hockey game, and the coach of the little guys team was wearing a T-shirt that read, "Mamas like good boys, but girls like bad boys." My first thought was that you should never trust the psychology you read on T-shirts. My second thought was that a lot of little hockey dudes are going to learn a not exactly accurate lesson from the coach's propaganda.

Your son is already somewhat compromised. He's been a chowhound for this kind of twisted input for years. Guaranteed. Listen to the comment of a famed media critic who recognized the power of slow, low-level persuasion: "If we are forced at every hour to watch and listen to horrible events, this constant stream of ghastly impressions will deprive even the most delicate among us of all respect for humanity."

That was Cicero, speaking in 80 B.C. Things haven't changed much since then. Neither have we. Today our sons are flooded with images that, though not ghastly, are just as able to make them lose respect for humanity. Images of girls in particular.

Pulling Up Porn by the Roots

Objectionable pictures, magazines, or computer files are easier than ever for young guys to get to. No matter how alarmed you might feel if they show up in your son's possession, remember that demonizing or humiliating him isn't much of a solution. He's a male human; he's floundering and highly distractible. Go easy. Actually, among boys, sharing porn is a communal thing, a bonding moment for boys, queer as that sounds.

Rather than respond immediately in disgust, take your time. Prepare yourself by praying, asking God's guidance, and asking that He show you how to proceed. You might talk things out thoroughly with a parent-adviser first.

When you do confront him, be direct and candid, letting him know you love and respect him—but not his choices. But tell him how finding those pictures makes you feel. Share with him the inappropriateness of having those pictures in the house and your need to eliminate their presence at the source. Let him know that if that means confiscating computer passwords or doing a book-bag check, so be it. Tell him you have no desire to be the police. The onus of change is on him.

Then start spending more time with him. Try to understand if his choices are part of a destructive pattern. Is he struggling with a sense of failure with the opposite sex? Is he lonely, in need of more human connections? Or is he just a dismayingly curious young male?

Rarely does a boy just run off and have sex with a girl. Many incremental steps are taken on this road. You might want to control the progress of many of these steps by disabling your television, monitoring and forbidding music that denigrates girls, and talking about the blitzkrieg of media messages that twist his values.

But whatever control steps you take, don't miss the most important one: You can help your young man learn how to see through propaganda.

It's a Jungle in There

So what do men really think about? The insights I'm going to discuss here are true and accurate. For the more reserved among you, they might be hard to hear. Be brave. Your son is learning them now. If you acknowledge them, you'll be able to more effectively inform your son about the realities he's experiencing, shape his attitudes and expectations, and help him get started toward a lifetime of healthy sexuality.

As long as I'm talking about taboos, let me add one more thought. Men have a burden to bear here that women don't. While both sexes can misuse their sexuality, men's sexuality—when expressed in a way that comes most naturally to them—is often considered fundamentally wrong. We're possessed by an obsession about sex yet asked not to act on it. You could say that while a woman has her sexuality, a man's sexuality has him. The world's reply to this urge is "Go for it!" The Bible's answer is different—accept it, be responsible, delay gratification, respect marriage, and value integrity and purity. Not to mention, keep your promises.

Four Simple Truths about Your Son's Sexuality

Immature sexual expression for men involves four not-so-flattering qualities: easy arousal, the thrill of the hunt, competition, and self-interest. Let's briefly look at each.

1. He's easily aroused. Everyone with a sexual appetite can occasionally be caught off guard by the strength of his or her urges. Sometimes sexual urges rise slowly, at other times very quickly. With young men, it's always fast. Teenage boys can get erections many times a day for no reason at all. I'm told that 95 percent of all young men masturbate, and the other 5 percent are liars. That lines up closely with my knowledge of guys. Their arousal can take as little as several seconds and can be prompted by something as insignificant as a glancing look by a girl, a close physical brush, or vibrations of the school bus. Every boy on the face of the earth is occasionally caught off guard by the strength of this beautiful urge.

2. He's obsessed with pursuit (even if it's only in his mind). Part of that instant urge might be called the "thrill of the hunt." The instinct to follow girls seems to be innate in guys. They do it almost unconsciously. It excites most guys. Until they mature and understand themselves better, they can easily make an obsession of following girls, secretly pursuing them, watching them, and dreaming of them. Of course, when they finally meet their "prey," they turn into a babbling geek. While his obsession is all reflex, his social skills must be learned.

3. He's curious and competitive. Guys are very competitive among themselves over sexuality. Women often make disparaging jokes about men and their gun belt notches, bedpost markers, and the like. But it's true that guys keep track of, rate, compare, and analyze their performance with girls. In short, they *compete*. I've found this to be true among both the awful guys I've known and among the best. It's not that men set out to devalue women; it's more that they're directed by some inner competitiveness to compare themselves to one another—and to win. They may need time, experience, and coaching to understand that aspects of this behavior are destructive.

4. He's self-interested. The sexual urges of young men (and often older men) are based almost entirely on self-interest. For an immature guy, sexual expression is for his own relief. A girl can easily be viewed as little more than a vehicle—a vehicle whose name, model, and year are irrelevant—and soon forgotten. Let me reiterate that teenage boys aren't manufacturing all these jungle impulses on purpose. They may look like insensitive animals, but they're not. They're just responding to something powerful, internal, and difficult to fathom. They don't sit around and try to dream up ways to use girls or compete for conquests in a blind attempt to satisfy their personal drives. They're just guys, and not very noble about it. And all their mothers' good lectures stop at the frontal lobes.

I hope that as you read these truths about guys that you don't get angry with them for what they begin life being. Rather, I hope that you will learn to work within these realities to help your son become a good man, able to rise to his incredible potential.

A Successful Loss of Innocence

Helping young men respect their sexual energy and learn to relate with girls begins with a flow of information. Sex and sexual urges must be talked about openly. Yet many parents keep silent about these powerful and obvious urges out of fear and ignorance. Scripture clearly teaches that we are fallen, weak creatures. In light of this, we need to develop a sense of bold confession, forgiveness, reanalysis, and commitment. Especially for fathers and sons, this happens by discussing our humanity in an atmosphere of helpfulness.

Your boy won't volunteer to do this. Take your time and bring these issues to the surface slowly. Our society is so flooded with sexual images it's easy to bring up these conversations almost anytime. The topics can be as wide-ranging as pornography, birth control, new physical changes, or the latest nude club to open in town with billboards as big as Connecticut. As you drive, go to movies, or watch television, the opportunities for spontaneous dialogue are wide open.

Sex in All the Wrong Places

You've intercepted a steamy note or a condom. What to do? First, remember that he may be completely chaste, just caught in a situation that looks bad. Give him the benefit of the doubt.

In private, present what you know graciously and straightforwardly. Don't expect him to tell you if he is having intercourse. But let him know that you care, why you care, and why you're watching. Hysteria won't get you far. Try "calm urgency." You'll be more likely to snare his sensibilities (he's feeling afraid and guilty) and lead him toward choosing responsibility, restraint, and abstinence.

Premarital intercourse has consequences that boys find easy to ignore or forget. Be prepared to offer some of your own methods and means of staying clear of ensnarements (the risks of inappropriate sex don't end with marriage). Teenage boys always seem stunned to be told that hanging out with the wrong girls is a sure way to get into the wrong situations—and a one-way ticket to a life he never wanted.

Have you been absolutely clear about your high expectations in this area? Have you made it plain that sexual self-control is possible? Does he know you're watching for telltale signs of sexual activity (evasiveness, cover-ups, keeping a relationship separate from family life, obsession with getting a girl alone).

Keep these conversations brewing. You're not trying to intimidate your son. You're taking risks to establish an open dialogue about things kids with hostile parents must be fearful or sneaky or frighteningly deluded about.

Every smart parent's first choice regarding a son's sexuality is this: talk. Talk when you're nervous. Use the amount of hair you have standing on end or the amount of perspiration that breaks out on your forehead as a "when to speak" guide.

Every smart kid's first choice? Don't talk. Your son probably doesn't trust you, especially with topics as touchy as sex. He probably has the strong feeling that something is wrong here, and it's better not to mention anything than to get busted. And I guarantee you, he believes that you cannot possibly understand how strong his sexual urges are and that you would crucify him if you did.

That's why we have to commit to traveling far outside our comfort zones speaking about sex, if we're to have any noticeable impact.

Talk. Let him know in small, constant ways that you are open to his natural development and that you're willing to discuss it. Notice his maturing body, ask him about his attractions to girls, mention that you heard him talking in his sleep (always guaranteed to flush a young man's face). It'll still take loads of time, but be patient.

When he does open up to talk, take it as an honor. It may happen anywhere, so respect his words, be discreet, and don't intentionally embarrass him *ever!* If you embarrass him, it may be the last time the two of you ever talk about this subject. Communicate that you're still a learner yourself and want to be as helpful as possible. This attitude, expressed over time, may just open him up to mature, information-building conversations.

Then again, it may all go nowhere. Be prepared to ask other adult men or women your son likes to join in your efforts to talk about sex and girls. Your son wants to talk, no doubt. What he needs to talk about may be more than you can give, so be aggressively open for good options. The girls in his life will thank you.

Relationship Building across the Gender Gap

Communication between the genders is crucial. A study I conducted for this book showed that fewer than 5 percent of boys feel as though they have even a slight understanding of the opposite gender. Boys are blind when it comes to communicating with girls. Several ideas might help you address this.

Girls mature much more quickly than boys. Just walk through a junior high school cafeteria at lunch sometime. The girls often look like the teachers. And the boys? Well, they look like boys. If they develop normally, most boys will catch up to the physical maturity of the girls by their senior year of high school.

A Closer Focus

Some Enchanted Prom Nights

Discuss the realities of magic evenings like prom night with your son. Maybe your "big night of the year" experiences were great, and maybe they weren't. Maybe they were pure bliss and fun, maybe a blur of foolish behavior, maybe you stayed home and looked in the mirror.

However they turned out, you owe it to your son to make the night special in a good way, not only for himself but for his date.

- Talk through plans for the evening so you're not in the dark.
- Find out what other kids are involved. (Do their parents know too?)
- Take the opportunity to help him plan how he spends his money. (More money doesn't always mean more fun or a happier date.)
- Let him know that magic evenings don't make family rules disappear.

This difference creates intense problems. Chief among them is that most boys generally feel intimidated in a girl's presence. Their experiential radar warns them that this other human being, this alien, is vastly different and in many ways superior. Competitive fires flare and mix with vague fears and the desire to be accepted. Then the whole combustible mix often fizzles into prickly, awful silence.

Over time, it can become a habit. And the vital life-links of communication can wither a bit and fail to grow and develop as they should.

But moms and dads can help. We can encourage an environment where teen men and women can mix socially with no performance requirements. Moms can help guys understand how to "decode" girl talk—about physical involvement and everything else. Dads can demonstrate how to make a woman feel both special and respected. No one wants to stand by and let these beautiful young men suffer inside their own clogged-up world.

Of course, they want parents to keep quiet and out of sight. They're afraid you will say something to embarrass them, that you will prove you are old and out of date, that you will prompt them to say something before they're ready. And you will. But don't let their paranoid demands stop you.

To begin fostering communication among the genders, review chapter 5, "Stealth Communication." It's loaded with useful ideas and techniques for opening the most stubborn communication jam. You might even suggest that your son read it if he needs some simple ideas for talking and interacting with others.

Conversational Catalysts

Some folks are really gifted as catalysts for conversation. Their trick is simple: Find commonalities among those they're with, then find reasons to bring those persons together. Social catalysts think about what they're asking and do what they can to create small, easy connections.

I have a friend who's a master at this. When I asked him about it, he told me that he doesn't really give it much thought. "Everybody has something in common," he said. "I'm just interested in finding out what it is." He doesn't try to be Oprah; he's simply interested in others and is courageous enough to begin asking questions that make small links.

A good place for gender linkages to happen is church youth groups. I firmly believe that this is one of the few places where effective cross-gender education can take place. Cross-sex interaction should be a high priority there.

How? It's actually easy once you understand that girls and guys desperately want to connect with and understand each other. They just don't have a format to do it. Since they naturally clump into gender groups anyway, your job can be as easy as spurring conversations between the teams. (Everyone feels safer in numbers.) If you ask their permission to pose hard questions or embarrassing topics, you'll almost always get guarded permission. With that permission, you can ask what you like.

Think of a list of interesting and controversial questions. Keep them on hand. For example:

- "Guys only want one thing, true or false?"
- "Why are girls so complicated emotionally?"
- "Does anybody have cool parents they can talk to?"
- "Why is the church so bossy about dating and sex?"

You can really have fun with this if you free yourself to ask dumb questions, naive or stereotyping questions, or thought-provoking questions. Remember, you want to foster communication between kids. It may be scary for some—but they'll line up if you decide to have another session.

Propose a "teen etiquette" night for your sons in which you coach them on the social fineries of how to treat and behave around girls. Teach by asking questions:

- "So, Eric, how would you introduce yourself to a girl you're really interested in? Show me..."
- "What are the basic good manners you should use when you're out on a date? Let's take it from before you pick her up to after you drop her off."
- "Pretend your date gets mud all over her pants. What would you do?"

Corny? Yes. But it works. When the chips are down and Buster is looking at this wonderful girl he'd love to introduce himself to, guess what he'll think about?

Knights in Shining Denim

Chivalry is making a comeback. Chivalry isn't about swordplay or jousting on horseback; the point of personal gallantry is to turn men into something special on behalf of women. The payoff for women is obvious. The payoff for your young man is self-confidence, success in relationships, and the lifelong pleasure that comes from helping others feel significant.

Encourage your son to take pride in saying nice things to and about girls. Teach him how to compliment a girl's strong points, her efforts to look nice and attractive, and her natural gifts. Remember, you're fighting a deeply ingrained tendency toward mistrusting girls. Your son is just a twitch away from a blind need to prove that all girls are wimps and he's the king of the jungle. So you'll need to lead by example.

Show him how to do thoughtful things for women and girls, especially in public. A young man's hit list:

- Think about what she might be needing (a drink? a warm wrap? a chair?) and offer to get it for her.
- Shield her from embarrassing or threatening situations and people.
- Speak well of her to others; introduce her to others if needed.
- Mind your eating, speaking, and escorting manners.
- Show genuine attention to what she has to say, and follow through with interested questions.
- Lock up those locker-room reflexes—bathroom jokes, coarse teasing, body noises—until you're off duty.

A Closer Focus

Attitude Adjustment

Over the next week, monitor how you and your spouse treat girls or women differently based on physical appearance. Consider these key situations:

- comments while watching TV or a movie
- comments in the mall
- gender-related smart remarks around the house to sister or Mom
- how you treat attractive females versus not-so-attractive ones

Turn your list into personal statements: "We equate beautiful with dumb," or, "We think pretty girls should get the benefit of the doubt." Think on it for a while because the attitudes you are communicating may not be what you really value or want your son to value. Write up a revised list of value statements—for example, "Attractiveness is great, but it has nothing to do with how well I treat a girl." Share it with your son. Help him to arrive at his own list; encourage him to write them down, and carry them on his person for a while.

Encourage him to notice when a girl needs his assistance. Encourage him to behave better than he might feel. Suggest he be willing to look a little foolish to save the honor of a girl (defending her reputation in a conversation; changing the subject if she's feeling awkward; deflecting attention if she's in a bad spot).

Encourage him to take a shower, clean his ears, brush his teeth, watch his complexion, use deodorant, and change his clothes every day. Moms especially make good prompters on matters of personal hygiene.

Encourage him to talk like a knight:

- "I like being with you."
- "You do that well."
- "Let me do that for you."
- "Really, it's OK. Don't worry about it."
- "Thanks for a great time."

Encourage him to give flowers.

These things are easy to do. A little prompting and suggesting on your part do a great deal of good. Apply yourself to it.

General kindness toward girls starts at home. In our home, all the steps toward chivalry start with the boys' sister and Mom. Most teenage boys need to be *compelled* to be kind to sisters, so roll up your sleeves. It's as vital a relationship as they'll ever have, but often one of the most contentious and difficult to reconcile. That's why we must devote attention to making it good.

Gentlemanliness with Adult Women

Here's the chance to let your boy really shine! I have told my sons many times that one of the keys to success in life is kindness and gentlemanliness to elders. As adults, we know just how powerful this is. Especially with adult women. There's something special about a young, polite gentleman. We have a responsibility to help our sons get there.

When I was a kid, I caddied at an exclusive club where politeness was more valued than proper yardage recommendations or club selection. The proprietor drilled me on etiquette, and though it came hard, those lessons have paid off tremendously in the intervening years. I learned to my surprise that "Yes ma'am," is as easy to say as a Neanderthal grunt.

I encourage my sons, when they're in the presence of a woman to:
- say "please" and "thank you"
- hold doors, pull out chairs, and offer other assistance
- eat last
- speak up and speak clearly when spoken to
- occasionally use "ma'am"
- smile and think up some intelligent questions to ask

At times, this training has nearly killed us all. But nobody ever said excellence was easy. It does, however, have its rewards. I cannot tell you how many women have told me my sons are a delight to be around. And they are.

Start off small. The next time you're going to be in the presence of an older woman (at a dinner gathering, for example, or at church), challenge your son to do one simple gentlemanly thing. Any of the suggestions on the above list will work. Ask him to do it as well as he can and then to watch the response. I guarantee that his gentlemanliness will be recognized and he will love it. And though he may not say it, he'll be grateful that you gave him the tools to be the toast of the kingdom.

In other words, to be an extraordinary young man.

Girls—Proving Ground for His Integrity

What starts with a rush of hormones in a guy ends up being perhaps the best opportunity to shape the inner man for greatness. And that's the way God meant it. Sex is certainly about keeping the species going. But in so many ways it can also be the fuel source of some of his greatest potentials. He has to learn to talk, he must strive to understand the opposite gender, he finds good reasons to harness his sexual passions, and he sets his sights on becoming an accomplished and desirable man of the world.

Every sexual longing and every relationship with a young woman is an opportunity for your son to recognize the importance of his integrity. Successful long-term relationships of any kind just don't happen without it.

Make sure your son knows that it's not OK to cheat, lie to, or mislead girls in relationships. Encourage him to be honest about the relationship—to be willing to struggle to articulate it for her and for himself. No girl deserves to be left in the dark or embarrassed in front of her friends. Instead of just not returning her calls, help your son to understand for himself, then to say to a young woman the hard truth.

One of the powerful benefits of teaching chivalry along with sex is that the outward behavior visibly reinforces the inward differences between guys and girls—how easy it is for a young man to tread on a girl's heart, to hurt or to heal her with his words. A real gentleman is true all the way through, and life will treat him better for it.

You don't need to look far to see that loose attitudes about sex and girls make titillating rap lyrics and blockbuster film plots. But they make for lousy relationships and miserable marriages.

What's the payoff for getting the girl-thing right? Boys who are healthy sexually and happy socially. That's something God can smile on.

Your son may see school as an enemy, a gauntlet of dubious value. He has difficulty seeing how what he's learning will help him. Remember the roles pain, pleasure, and curiosity have with your young man?

- School is all pain, and the long-term goal (income, security, careers) is shrouded in adult jargon.
- School brings little pleasure. It can't compete with a car, a video game, a new CD by Rage Against the Machine, a girl, or a double bacon cheeseburger with fries.
- School only rarely hooks his curiosity. What exactly do Charlemagne, passive verbs, and cosine curves have to do with the swirl of life inside his head?

Your son faces another problem specific to guys: Strong academic competitors often get labeled as nerds and are shunned. That's why it's common, especially in the early and mid-teens, for guys to keep their grade levels and interest levels just below the line of sight. To your son, being cool is more important than being smart.

Recruiting a Winning Team

A parent's challenge is to accept the realities of school for young men while reaching for provocative responses that will make school too tantalizing and vital for them to pass up. You can do that by creating a team of people properly oriented toward your son's academic achievement.

You can create a winning team by first getting to know all the players involved. Many players compete in your son's educational game. The most obvious player is your son, who receives 95 percent of your academic attention. But there are three others: you, your son's teachers, and your son's school. Four groups of players, all with different agendas and plans, all with some power, and all hopefully—but almost never—well aligned.

Your son was made to learn and grow, and he wants to do that. His curiosities drive him hard, and given the right orientation, he's capable of learning many new things. In chapter 2 I described seven intellectual gifts that your son has, in varying degrees:

- Artistic intelligence
- Logic or mathematical intelligence
- Spatial intelligence
- Musical intelligence
- Physical intelligence
- Interpersonal intelligence
- Intrapersonal intelligence

Your son excels at, and gets very excited about, at least one of these. For example, though his understanding and mastery of trigonometry might be zilch, he might be very interested and excited about Rembrandt

A Closer Focus

Pick a Teacher's Brain

With your son's permission, set up a meeting with his favorite teacher. Your objective is to get to know the teacher's personality, teaching style, and feelings about his or her subject. Your son will be shocked and impressed by your curiosity. And you may come away with answers to these questions that can be important keys to your son's academic success: Is my son driven by relationship or performance? How does he respond to challenge? What learning environment works best for him? How can I apply this information in my parenting?

or Bach or counseling fellow classmates. It all depends on the combination of your son's strengths in these seven areas.

Each boy is born with a different combination. To create an effective learning environment that supports and encourages your son, be sensitive to what excites his curiosities and causes his mental gears to creak to life.

One player often ignored in your son's educational game is *you*. The baggage you carry from your own expectations and experiences can be a help or a hindrance. Properly balanced expectations and demands can bring out the best in him. There's no magic formula for finding that balance, but it begins with a simple reevaluation of yourself.

Do you expect great scholastic performance because you want him to do well? Or do you push it because you were an underachiever and it cost you? Is his performance more about your pride and reputation? Your answers here don't matter as much as being honest with yourself.

Don't overanalyze. Just ask yourself some simple questions:

- Am I jealous of really smart people?
- Is the world biased in favor of smart people?
- Do I look down on people who aren't very bright?
- Did I have any really great teachers?
- Could I have tried harder in school?
- Did I let my own stubbornness ruin my grades?

Be especially on guard if your experiences and attitudes have made your home academically hostile. You help create this when:

- you condemn schools or teachers ("The schools are a total waste, and all teachers are overpaid!")
- you encourage mediocrity ("If you can get away with it, do it.")

- you imply that certain teachers are rubes ("Hey, if you can outsmart the teacher, why not?")
- you have a lazy attitude toward education yourself ("I want you to get A's—now bring me my beer and my remote!")
- you excessively tease about grades or brightness ("You're stupid, just like that flunky, Uncle Harry.")
- you make unreasonable demands ("I want straight A's, or else.")

Another group of players are the *teachers*. Get to know them and communicate with them regularly. You can't realistically grade them without understanding who they are and how they do their job.

Great teachers can be found everywhere, and you must know if your son has some. Great teachers are passionate about their subject (which creates excitement), relaxed but in control, tough without being cruel, willing to teach, and patient.

A teen's mom or dad can be a continual advocate for teaching quality. Search for talented, dedicated teachers in your son's school and encourage him to sign up for quality learning experiences instead of popularity or easy grades. And encourage his teachers in practical ways. Encouragement makes them better teachers and more effective members of your son's educational team.

The last player is the *school system* itself. Try to ascertain what the school's objectives really are. Sometimes a school's stated objectives sound great, but its actual objectives are quite different. For instance, a school might *say* it's committed to the students when it's really focused on meeting budgets, protecting the seniority system, or keeping the employees' union happy. If you attend even a few school functions with your son, you'll bump into the right people to ask and watch.

Also, the telephone can be a great friend. Schools that are deeply committed to the kids welcome input and questions from parents. Unless a school is jaded from years of trouble, lack of discipline, and general mayhem, those who run the school will usually respond quickly to your telephone inquiries.

Schools are run by people, and people respond to helpfulness, kindness, thoughtful suggestions, and encouragement. You can't change everything. And sometimes you need to take radical, corrective measures for your son's best interest. But get involved first, and get tough last. In most cases excessive force is counterproductive.

School Rules Start at Home

Whether your son wants to drive a tractor for a living, buy out Intel, play pro ball, or be a pastor in Papua, New Guinea, right now school should be his number-one priority. To help accomplish this, you will need to be at your provocative best. I suggest you set up an attention-getting system and stick by it.

Let your son know that failure is not an option. When I say *failure* here, I'm talking about not failing in the things he can control. Attendance, for example, is something your son can usually control.

A Closer Focus

Making the Grade

Performing well at school is a teenager's "life work." After he graduates, he can have his pick of another goal. But in adolescence, good grades are job #1. Our demands are simple: Do your best and aim for A's. If you put in hours of studying and can't accomplish that, that's fine, but don't quit shooting high. At our house, at least a half-hour per night is devoted to reading books, and all the kids are responsible to keep us posted accurately about their school progress.

It's not optional. He can control the outcomes of tests only minimally—but he can control homework, preparation for tests, and attitudes about their importance.

If necessary, set up a daily schedule, location, and working conditions (no headphones for example) for him to accomplish his homework. You're not a nagging mother when you do this; you're his manager (every good rock band has one). You're not an overbearing dad when you insist on a winning game plan and rigorous workouts; you're his head coach. (Where would Joe Montana have been without Bill Walsh?)

A final note: Good grades always come before jobs, sports, extracurriculars, friends, or play.

Show him his team. Help your son see that since you play a major part in his education, you're prepared to meet him halfway. This is provocative parenting in action. Think about what help you're willing to offer. ("If your alarm fails to go off, I'll wake you." "If you're failing algebra, I'll quiz you nightly." "I'll talk to your teachers at least once a semester." "If you need tutoring, I'll pay.") Try to make your halfway offers positive and not drudgery.

Since every kid is different, success is achieved differently. Whatever the path or whatever your son's academic ability is, make his success a team effort. The teacher isn't the enemy; neither are the lousy school lunches. A failure to learn is the enemy. So is a loss of freedom later in life—and failure status now. But your son is fortunate enough to have a team around him. And they're all playing hard for him.

Keep his eyes on the goal. Parents who are oriented toward higher goals ask their sons, "Are you learning to think? Are you training your curiosity? Are you using self-discipline? Are you getting skills and self-confidence? Do you understand the purpose behind the assignment?"

Make school pay. Considering that school is your son's job, should he get benefits? Parties, bonuses, days off, comp time, retirement? Seems fair to me, and if your son knows that you're prepared to express your inner pride in tangible ways, he's more likely to pull hard.

The Real Core Curriculum

Imagine that there are two curriculums in your son's school, the paper one in the guidance counselor's file cabinet and the internal one your son takes into his future. Guess which one prevails in the long run?

It's the learning priorities in his head that really matter. He can forget all about Charlemagne, passive verbs, and cosine curves and do just fine. (He can relearn those data over a pizza anytime he needs them.) But the real priority of education is *the quality of young man your son is becoming in the process of his school success.*

As parents, we can be looking for ways to track how our sons are doing in this larger curriculum. For example, we can ask:

- How well is my son doing at developing the basics—responsibility, test taking, organizational habits, etc.?
- What is he learning about people, both peers and those in authority?
- How about his character and values?

With this in mind, let's try to describe the real core curriculum that we should be managing purposefully.

Basic Job Performance 101

These are the basic skills drilled throughout secondary education: personal organization, study habits, thinking and concentration skills, and test-taking skills, plus abiding by basic school requirements of attendance and campus behavior. Let's add the learned skills of getting up every morning in time to get to school and turning in every night at a sensible time.

Some parents stumble on the basics. I've heard dads say, "Hey, it's his life. If he won't get up on time, that's his problem." But the team approach says, "Hey, we're all going to take a hit if you don't do your part. Your part is getting out of bed when the alarm goes off. Here's what I'm willing to do (Are you sitting down?) to help you take honors at it..."

This may be where you'll have to be at your provocative best:

Be audaciously present. I know one mom who spent a day going to all of her son's classes. He'd been suffering from the truancy virus. Her attendance subtly told the young man's classmates, "Sorry guys, Danny still needs a baby-sitter."

Get a better metaphor. School isn't jail. Maybe for your crowd-pleasing son it's a stage. (Help him figure out how to use his high school career to master skills like public speaking, acting, leadership, musical performance, etc.) Maybe for your young hacker, straight A's are a ticket to the 200-megahertz machine of his dreams.

Get a better idea. Get your auditory son a Dictaphone for recording lectures and reading homework aloud. If your son isn't getting his homework done in his room, set him up on the dining room table without benefit of music or phone.

Provoke change. Let him spend time around those who have refused to take school seriously (a job in a wrecking yard? volunteering at a downtown mission? a visit to juvenile detention?). Conversely, let him see the benefits of success (a day at a TV studio? a campus visit to a college or professional school? reading an autobiography of an inspiring person he admires?).

Have fun. For some of us, fun is the easy part. For others, it's the easy-to-overlook part. Here are just a few starters:

- Make fun happen for your son *at school.* Send him tickets to a concert there. Build on the party-possibilities of school events. Pick him up for a quick lunch.
- Give him "one day off for outstanding achievement" coupons. Let the school know what you're up to.
- Make your home the place he and his friends can come to study or to just hang out.

Friends and Other Distractions 201

Peer acceptance is a strong part of a teen boy's curriculum. The power exerted by peers is enormous. Like all people, teenage boys naturally attempt to become like those they want to be around. The motives for those choices are complex, but on the surface they're simple: Teenagers try to blend in with their pals and avoid distinction at all costs.

My brother-in-law, Matt Godsil, is a high school teacher and master of teenagers. He calls this process "peer fear." He thinks teenagers aren't so influenced by peers as they are afraid of standing alone. Terror enters the heart of any teenage boy who suddenly feels he's alone and about to be ostracized for any reason—a belief, a good grade, a bad haircut.

That feeling of aloneness is too much for most teens, and they'll quickly bow to peer fear by rushing to anonymity. In many cases this isn't so bad. It can teach teens how to blend in at work and in social settings. But our boys also can get "peer-feared" into wrong attitudes and actions.

To help my sons (who staunchly believe they're independent and above the influences of their buddies) avoid this trouble, I illustrate how they are the average of their peers in almost all respects.

Since my peers affect me, too, I use myself as an example. I predicted that my financial income would be the average of my five closest friends. We did the numbers (guessing my friends' incomes) and sure enough, it was very close. Then we tried the average game using their peers' grades, income, car insurance rates, amount of free time and study time, and extracurricular involvement. The results were sobering.

I urged them to put the averaging principle to work for them:

- If they want to feel better about themselves, find happier people.
- If they want to get ahead, hang with people who are moving on.
- If they're tired of being followers, hang with leaders.
- If they want to earn more money, hang with people who earn more money.

Two particularly virulent kinds of people can drop the averages in your son's life. First are the negative people, the naysayers. Second and worse are the naysayers who are also blackmailers and will penalize others if they refuse to join in the misery. Your teenager is probably susceptible to both, though he's unaware of them. His senses are probably dull to their "atti-cide"—the killing of his attitude.

When I discuss peer choices with my kids, I talk about my own friends and acquaintances. I rub shoulders with some negative people; this is not good, but it's real. And I can be honest with my boys about my own personal susceptibility to peers who can hurt me. I've even asked my kids to help me monitor "negs" who've infiltrated my camp. We rate people's attitudes on a ten-point scale. Believe me, my sons are always happy to show me when I'm slipping into the clutches of a negative thinker.

After you get your son to point out the negative people in your life, make an agreement: If they can make observations about your friends, you can make the same observations about theirs. OK, it's a sneaky move but fair. They shouldn't mind as long as they know you're not trying to rip their pals and you confine your comments to problem-solving suggestions.

Strategies for Personal Growth 301

In this part of the curriculum, your son should be learning how to think about and decide who he'll be. He needs to be developing personal success habits and maturity. This includes building self-confidence, motivation, and self-discipline. I recommend that you make sure your son is receiving practical encouragement and practice in his spiritual growth as well.

Our sons need to be prepared to handle the really brutal tests in life—people and situations that will trip them into failure if they haven't built a strong character to go with their classroom knowledge or performance.

One thing our family does is to give our kids access to motivational speeches via videos and personal appearances by some of our generation's great speakers. I'm associated with The People's Network (TPN), a personal-development-and-motivation television channel on satellite.

A Closer Focus

Life in the Rumor Factory

High schools are rumor factories—places where hundreds of young minds without enough creative outlets imagine and spread all manner of hearsay and innuendo. The gossip is so rampant your son might learn to believe rumors more than facts.

Help your son learn to sift fantasy from facts, opinions from facts, hearsay from facts, jumped-to conclusions from facts, credible sources' powerful testimony from facts… Gossip and rumors really do end up hurting others and damaging friendships (see Proverbs 17:9).

TPN's corporate goal is to bring positive television into homes around the world. It does this by providing the world's greatest motivational speakers, teachers, coaches, and authors the opportunity to teach and encourage.

My kids watch the channel routinely, and on many occasions I've heard them repeat phrases and statements of optimism, encouragement, and vision I know came from what they heard.

Motivational speakers have a tremendous impact on my kids. Whether the topic is sports, business, or Christian living, these speakers are trained to speak simply, practically, and with tremendous emotional impact. My boys are fascinated by people who are so publicly positive. And they remember what's been said.

This channel can change your home. How much would you pay to hear your son say, "If it is to be, it's up to me"?[1]

Power Moves 401

Learning to relate well with elders and those in authority is one of life's most important lessons. That education begins in kindergarten. But you can foster that process by showing and coaching your son on how to recognize power relationships.

In high school, teenagers begin to sense that authority doesn't come from physical size or age alone. Your son may have to relearn who has power and influence and why he should treat that person with appropriate respect. The big guy in the back row who gets a laugh when he calls the teacher stupid in class is likely to be the same one who gets laughed at when he applies for a good job.

Our sons need to be learning that respect for authority goes a long

---

[1] For more information on this service, contact Bill Beausay at bbeausay@aol.com.

way on this planet. Consider the persons in power your son will have
to learn to live successfully with:

- teachers, counselors, administrators, janitors, coaches
- law-enforcement officers and those in the judicial system
- employers, managers, and other bosses
- college and graduate-school teachers and administrators
- security personnel
- any person or company he owes money to
- elders

It only works to thumb your nose at the world if you're not planning to enjoy your visit. Respect is not the same as manipulation or
"sucking up." It's a recognition of our dependence on another and the
honor that is due that person.

Help your son learn to write thank-you notes, speak deferentially
and politely to others, and value a good reputation (and a glowing job
reference).

The Future Switch 501

The purpose of school is to prepare our sons for their tomorrows. The
problem is that teenagers are stuck in today, have only a vague sense of
time passing, and behave as if they'll live forever.

The fact is that in the world that awaits my boys there won't be detention hall, only docks in pay and few retakes, only getting passed over for
someone who got it right the first time. We must keep setting up experiences with the future for our young men; otherwise they may easily
flunk this important part of school (even while getting straight A's now).

Here are practical steps we parents can take to help our sons:

- Keep talking about what kind of future they want.

- Make sure that they're keeping up with course requirements, college applications, and admissions tests.
- Let them try on many options without shaming them for being confused or indecisive.
- Let them know at every opportunity that we believe in their gifts and their promising life ahead.

One priority at our home is to try to put our sons into close proximity with those who are doing what they see themselves doing in the future. We support this in any way possible—visits, introductions, reading, movies, and phone conversations. A boy deserves the chance to learn about possible directions by watching, asking, and participating before he has to decide. And learning what he dislikes is just as valuable. If he learns that spending his days looking at someone's cavities *isn't* what he wants, then at least he can rule out dental school. It's better to find that out at sixteen than at thirty-six.

One dad I know uses car time to interview his boys about their likes and dislikes:

- "Would you rather work alone or in a group? Inside or outside? With your hands or with your mind? In one place or moving around?"
- "Would you rather be in charge or not in charge?"
- "Do you like competition better or getting along better?"
- "Would you rather have money or reputation?"
- "Would you rather have low potential with low risk of failure or high potential with high risk of failure?"

A conversational tool I use with teenagers is to ask them to treat their futures like a picture. Ask questions like: "Where's the future?" "Can you point to it?" "What does it look like?" "Is anyone else there that you've met before?" "Do they look happy?"

Help Them Graduate a Little Every Day

You could say that a big part of schooling is a transfer of ownership: Your son's future is being transferred from you and his teachers into his own hands. You want your son to own his education, whether that education is a world tour or enrollment at the local community college. Ownership comes with understanding what it could be, wanting it, and setting about to get it.

His stepping up to take possession of his school obligations, his money, his transportation, his lodging, and all of his other needs and desires happens in a successful progression from childhood to full emancipation.

We need to help our sons graduate a little bit every day. Education is the key to your son's future freedom and to winning. This holds true whether your son ends up working in the trades, the professions, or in business.

Boys may hate school, but they love their freedom. And they're crazy about winning. We'll know we've gotten an A+ as a parent when our boys start to see every pop quiz and cranky teacher as their ticket to the life of their dreams.

Because they would be right.

Chapter Eleven

Touchdowns and Jam Sessions

The power of music and sports

Your name totally rocks!"

Not long ago my son was playing an interactive chesslike game on the Internet. His partner was some female cyberstranger, clearly his superior at the game. She was so quick, in fact, that she'd make her move, then type in her flirts on a separate screen while he pondered his play. He hardly talked to her and seemed put off by her incessant questions and remarks.

At the time he was using the screen name "Dig-it" to identify himself. He got that handle off the lyrics to a song he liked. As it happened, his game opponent was giddy about the name. She kept typing in, "That name totally rocks!"

Finally she got around to asking him one of the big questions: "Do you like such-and-such band?" (She knew the lyrics, too, and liked the same band.)

Next thing you know, my son had dropped the game and was deep into a type-fest with his new cyberfriend about the band. The girl had nailed his hot button. They blabbed on. Soon I realized that the interactive game was over. Music, not strategy, was the hit.

Voyaging on the Sea of Emotion

This incident reminded me of a valuable lesson: A teen's hot buttons and passions are the gateways to his heart. Other kids use them. Why not parents?

We've spent a great deal of time looking at why the teenage years are so intense for your son. The answer lies in an understanding of his burgeoning brain development and the abstract thinking abilities this permits. These new capabilities may result in spells of withdrawal, new social awareness, a search for a new identity, and emotional defenses that few can penetrate.

Parents are often the first to be shut out. If you wish, you can argue with your teenage son about his emerging priorities, tastes, ignorance, obsessions—but you'll probably lose.

Not long ago I got into a debate with some teenage guys who had gathered on my front porch. Thinking back on it now, I don't even remember what it was about. All I recall is that the collective illogic of these boys was amazing. I had them tied in logic knots in under sixty seconds.

But I lost. The conversation ended suddenly when they started drifting away. I learned an important lesson that day: *You can think deeper than your son, but you can't feel deeper.* You can tolerate losing your son's head, but don't lose his heart. If you lose his heart, you've lost something much more important than some argument or point of wisdom.

As the guys left my porch that day, I felt empty. Yes, they think and decide with their heads, but they live with their hearts.

Adolescence is about new, deep, swirling combinations of pleasure and pain. We need to find a way to ply these deep waters and navigate them successfully. We need boats. The odd match of music and sports are very effective schooners.

Two Pillars of Adolescence

An old mentor of mine once explained what struck me as a profoundly simple way of looking at life. He told me that life was founded on four "pillars." The four pillars are work, play, the arts, and mystery. A good life, he suggested, is equal parts of all four. He urged me to put forth equal effort developing and pursuing each area. Those words illuminated my path and are responsible for many of the things I value today.

Teenage males in America are simpler. For most of them, there are only two pillars that matter: the arts and play. And translated, that often means "music and sports."

Actually, music and sports touch us all. Who doesn't perk up and listen at the sound of a tune? The deep thump and bash of a drum set? The sweet purr of a violin? Who doesn't feel a pulse of excitement hearing football players in the park yell and laugh as they play hard? A buzz of adrenaline from hearing a crowd cheering? The draw is so utterly reliable, we sophisticated people-builders can turn it to *our* strategic advantage with our teens.

I recommend marrying the odd couple. You may think discussing music and sports in the same chapter is strange, but discussing the two together actually makes a lot of sense. For your young man, music and sports both effectively serve to:

- get his mind off his own troubles
- help him feel better about himself (he's good at something; he's a fan, "an insider")
- channel, express, and relieve his often overwhelming emotions
- give him a label, an identity at a time when he's looking for one

Frankly, I'm interested in any simple solution that provides all these benefits and creates a natural point of alliance.

Remember that the person with a system always controls the person without one (chapter 3). Blend that with the reality that nothing works better with young men than being audaciously present, and you've got the chemistry for lots of fun.

First, let's explore ways we can use the drawstrings of music to pull us all closer together.

Making Connections through Music

Music is as diverse as we are. The types are nearly endless: rock music, blues, rap, jazz, contemporary Christian music, folk music, country music, classical music, heavy metal, fifties, sacred, Irish music—why, even Bulgarian throat music! It calls us to great heights and pulls us to deepest depths. Sometimes it simply entertains. Other times it impassions us. It can repulse or violate. And it never seems to be any better than the heart, mind, and talents of the musician making it. Using a few simple strategies, you can find music a very effective relational and parenting tool.

Listen up. You need to be involved, "audaciously present" in your son's musical experience, whether he's a performer or a consumer. When I say this to groups of parents I usually draw a big groan. I'm not asking you to like his music, though you may be one of the blessed parents who has a son with similar musical tastes. But at least once, sit down and listen to his music. If he'll let you, do it with him. Show him that you are willing to entertain the distant possibility that you might love what he loves.

Try to find something good to say about his preferences. If you're like me, this will be hard. I'm a jazz guy, and I value creativity and complexity. House-thundering noise just makes my teeth hurt. When I listen to it, I feel like I swallowed a firecracker. Obviously, my kids can't relate. Teeth-chattering volume is exactly what they love. And that's OK.

Ask your son to take you on a guided tour of his favorites—lyrics and music. Ask if he minds your offering comments or asking questions. Most teenage men are delighted to accommodate a curious tourist.

Not long ago my son and I went to hear one of his favorite bands in concert. I happen to like this band a bit, so my participation wasn't a big deal. What struck me, though, was not even so much what happened at the concert (which by my sixties standard was pretty tame) but how Jake treated me once he realized I would go with him. The fact that I was even willing to attempt it suddenly set me apart from all the other boring, father stereotypes in his mind. That in itself was worth the effort.

Ask questions. Tell him you are interested in his music, and being a thoughtful person, you may have a question from time to time. Secure his permission to ask it. He'll say yes.

You may also want to ask for a copy of the lyrics so you can follow along. If the lyrics are bad, bawdy, or screamed, you'll have trouble getting them. But ask anyway. I can guarantee your son has all the lyrics memorized down to the breathiest, most inaudible "umm-ooh-yeah."

A Closer Focus

Tune In

Have a DJ night. Every family must play a favorite song that captures, in a tune, something important about him or her—a true feeling, a memory, a story. It's sort of embarrassing. But everyone learns something and leaves with a greater appreciation of why some family members like Pearl Jam and others Itzhak Perlman.

Appreciate that asking him to explain lyrics might make him a bit uncomfortable. Once I noticed that whenever I walked into my son's room he'd immediately start talking over the music. I wasn't born yesterday. "What's this guy screaming about?" I asked. He shot me that look that begged for thumbscrews rather than having to fess up. But I kindly persisted, and the conversation that followed was one of the most memorable we've ever had.

Teenage boys love being the authority on things parents know nothing about. You can seize a tremendous communication advantage here by occasionally "playing dumb" and letting your son express his intellect. I can't tell you how many times I've simply acted like I was crossbred with a turnip, only to have my sons excitedly jabber on about things they were the relative experts on.

Ask how your son's music influences him. Most teens really don't believe the music they like influences them much. This is not a defensive denial on their part, just a naive assumption about their own invulnerability. Music can move them imperceptibly, and they need to be made aware of it. Your discussions will unwrap the secrecy of what your son is listening to and help him respond more sanely.

Share a musical influence from your life—a lyric or a phrase from a song that really speaks to you. Talk about catchy tunes that get stuck in your head.

What's the value of a conversation like this? Long-term connections. Laying the groundwork for future conversations. Improving trust and reliability between you two. Perhaps moving the musical junk out of the closet into the light.

Get informed. I don't want to torture you, but I suggest you take the minutes required to read CD jacket information, keep one eye on the music-scene column in your local paper, and track the music and musician reviews in *People* magazine. I've found that my sons really appreciate my willingness to at least be minimally informed. It costs so little, and the payoffs in credibility are hard to overestimate.

Teaching Values and Character in 4/4 Time

Whoever dreamed up the phrase "face the music," didn't know he or she was giving some great parenting advice. With today's breakdown in restraints, music for the young provides many great teaching opportunities. We must try to face the music with our sons to keep them on key for life.

Make your consumer requirements clear. Let's keep all our parental worries in proper perspective. To be candid, I'm a lot more worried about my kids' driving than about their music. However, I think it's wise to create a playlist of rules within your home. Every family with teenage music consumers deserves one. For example:

- We belong to Jesus Christ—no music is OK that blatantly glorifies death, Satan, or the occult.
- We respect women, marriage, and sexual morals.
- We don't use music to condone hatred of others.

A Closer Focus

Head Music

Wearing headphones in a social setting—even the family living room—is disrespectful unless your teen asks first. Sometimes earphones are just earphones, no offense intended. They spare adults from noxious tastes in sound and give our kids privacy—like on trips, while studying, or during quiet moments around the house. But make sure they don't turn into sonic baby-sitters or relationship twilight zones. Being plugged into tunes is a blast, but being plugged into family is the best.

- We are open to quality music in all its expressions.
- We value creating music as much as consuming it.

These are guidelines parents can verbalize to let kids know what's OK to play around the house. In the long run, probably the most important element is that you are simply taking a stand. Not a particularly offensive or restrictive one either.

Before you see red, look for gold. You've no doubt had the experience of hearing a song your son likes, not being able to quite pick out the words, and straining to listen carefully. Then you hear it and wish you hadn't. Or perhaps you're cleaning a room and find a CD you wished you hadn't found. Or maybe you walk into your son's room and find a new poster that has less to do with music than with creating a tinge of pleasure.

As much as possible, use those moments for teaching, not screaming.

Coalitions between you and your son are built over time. Rarely are they made or broken over one incident. Therefore don't judge yourself too harshly if you've seen red and blown up before. Next time go for the gold. Borrowing some lessons from chapter 5, avoid "why?" questions as they can seem to *require* a defensive answer. Instead ask questions like, "How did you think I'd respond?" or "What does this say about you?"

Try to leverage the conversation to some place more golden than just another shootout.

Offer alternatives. Such a wide variety of music is available in our world, do both of you a favor and develop alternatives. The Christian music scene is exploding with better quality and fresh styles of music.

Use your son's musical interests to nudge him toward:

- related books, collections, and autobiographies
- spiritual growth, arts, drama, or film

- investing in his future—performance, scholarships, new
  instruments, and lessons

One night my sons and I spontaneously got out our two favorite, all-time songs and played them for each other. It was a great time, and we all had a chance to give feedback and discuss what different artists were trying to express. No matter how musically sophisticated a teenager happens to be, there's lots of music he's never heard. Borrow music from the library. Much of it you'll dislike, but take a chance and find out where it goes.

Being able to play a musical instrument is a healthy, socially interactive, artistically productive thing to do. Encourage it.

Affirm the Value of Gusto

Be on guard against what I fear is the deepest problem with all this. It's a problem C. S. Lewis so ably pointed out in *The Screwtape Letters*. The biggest trap awaiting us in this life is not evil impulses, but no impulses. Emptiness is the most virulent type of ungodliness. Unfortunately, some of the music of this generation leaves listeners feeling empty.

Value innocence, because innocence allows your teenager to feel strong passion. Some level of youthful naiveté prevents him from feeling jaded or cynical, which in turn provides the basis for hope. Where there is hope, there is passion. Where there is passion, there is life!

Help your son feel passionately—one way or the other—about what he hears. Encourage him not to wallow in the lukewarm middle ground of apathy that so much pop music seems driven to create. Miracles are always possible among people who feel deeply, but not much will ever happen for kids stuck in numbness. Music can be a God-given gateway to excellence and caring and living.

Staying in the Game with Sports

We've overemphasized the value of sports in this country, but at the same time we've surely underemphasized the value of using sports to create connections with our kids. Remember, for teenage guys, talking and relating are what you do *while* you're having fun (like shooting baskets, hitting golf balls, or tuning a motocross engine). Many kinds of sports and games offer provocative potential for alert parents:

- family recreational activities (biking, splatball, road-rally racing)
- inside games (billiards, video games, chess)
- competitive sports (running, climbing, swimming)

For the purposes of this chapter I'm going to focus on competitive and recreational sports. Why? Several reasons. First, your son is full of energy and needs a release. Teenage boys love to test themselves, to win. And you probably sit too much and need to get out too.

Sports are "plug-and-play" fun. You don't really have to be playful or even creative because the sport itself provides the thing to do—you just plug yourself in and go, as either a participant or a spectator. Consider the options (categories are somewhat arbitrary):

- Water—boating, jet-skiing, water-skiing, crew (rowing), swimming, canoeing, fishing
- Engines and speed—motorcycle riding/racing, auto racing/ rallying
- High-aggression, strength—boxing, rugby, football, martial arts, wrestling, weightlifting
- Finesse—soccer, baseball/softball, basketball, fencing, gymnastics, handball, tennis, billiards, volleyball, rifle/pistol shooting, badminton, table tennis, platform tennis

- Winter and bad weather, indoors—snowmobiling, ice hockey, roller hockey, luge/tobogganing, figure skating, skiing (downhill and cross-country), bowling, curling
- Endurance—running, bicycling
- Other outdoor sports—horseback riding/showing/steeplechasing, Rollerblading, surfing, scuba diving, archery, hunting, golf, croquet, horseshoes, shuffleboard

All of these sports offer relationship-building opportunities for different kinds of parents and sons. But there are some basic attitudes that will help you transform these activities from plain opportunities for expending money and sweat into memorable man-building experiences.

Express interest. Don't miss this stroke of genius. Expressing interest in what your son is interested in is a powerful, nonverbal affirmation. Your son will be flushed with a warm appreciation that you are interested (though don't hold your breath waiting for him to ever say it).

Once my son came home with a snowboard he picked up at a neighbor's garage sale. This was several years ago, before the craze, and nobody really knew what to do with it. Not being terribly afraid of toys, I offered to go with him to check it out. We had quite a time figuring out how to ride that rascal without injuring body or pride. And neither of us escaped carnage. But did we ever have fun! Bruises never felt so good. And my son is still impressed that I gave it a try.

Participate enthusiastically. Don't just be there. Remember—be audaciously present. Be the parent who yells, who cheers—not just for your boy, but for his whole team. What costs you little by way of showing emotions goes a long way toward filling up his emotional tank. Showing excitement might be risky for your temperament, but it's almost always the right thing to do. And it's contagious.

Get informed. Bone up on the star athletes in a sport your son loves. Memorize a few favorite statistics of his favorite players or teams, then see the reaction you draw when you cite them. His jaw will hit the potato-chip bowl. A little information goes a long way to prompting conversations and deepening respect.

When I was a counselor, I found that thirty seconds of research in the daily box scores and individual stats made me sound like Yogi Berra. The young counselees I saw always perked up and chattered like birds when I opened with the latest numbers.

Playing Your Way to Character Strengths

In my first book, *Boys! Shaping Ordinary Boys into Extraordinary Men*, I wrote that sports have great potential but, like television, have fallen into the wrong hands. But we don't have to give up in disgust. We should ask ourselves, Is my son a better person for having participated in organized sports? If the answer is yes, keep him in. But if it's no, be honest and clear about it.

As a motivational trainer, I know that your son will never have a safer and more effective environment than sports to shape the success attitudes of champions. Organized play teaches:

- what it takes to win
- how to lose and come back from "failure"
- how to manage tempers, conflict, and intense competition
- the code of good sportsmanship
- how to be coachable
- perseverance (never quit)
- no pain, no gain

When a mom or dad looks at that list of traits, it's hard to take sports lightly. What course at school or even church could guarantee the same high-impact curriculum? Let's examine these strength benefits one at a time:

The Winning Attitudes of Champions

Most of us have never had the experience of being a champion. We're only vaguely aware of what champions need to endure and push through in order to reach the top.

What are some of those? First, they believe they can win. They believe that the next play will score a touchdown, the next service will be an ace, the next several feet of rockface will put them on a better line up the mountain.

Second, they have a plan to win. They know what they're going to do.

And third, they're willing to endure pain and discomfort to see the plan through.

Sports can provide a reasonably protected arena where our young

---

A Closer Focus

Coaches, Bosses, and Other Maestros

A good coach or boss can be very beneficial to your son in terms of career advice, future job referrals, sources of future business contacts, etc. A bad one can be the source of endless wisdom about how not to conduct a life. Your son has to learn to use that relationship properly.

The relationship may need some tutoring from you. If the boss or coach is particularly bad (demeaning, harsh, critical, unfair, unresponsive), encourage your son to move on. Perseverance has limits, and a boss or coach who is damaging on purpose due to some sort of twisted personal management style does not deserve an hour of your son's life.

men can learn these attitudes—and allow them to be instilled, tested, and matured.

Learning to Lose

Young men need to learn how to lose. They don't have to like it—and probably shouldn't. But they must learn how to endure its ego pain (and often physical pain)—then get up and push on.

An atmosphere where both encouragement and acceptance are plentiful makes all the difference. I recently read a research study suggesting that people who are verbally encouraged by others can endure nearly twice the pain as those who have no encouragement. Your son's coach and his teammates are investing significantly in his future well-being.

Managing Tempers and Conflict

Sports participation teaches boys to control their tempers even when emotions are running high. The unwritten rules of sports etiquette require players to maintain composure in harsh, embarrassing, and sometimes humiliating situations.

These unwritten rules—such as, it's not cool to cry if someone slam-dunks a basketball over your head, or it's not proper to run up and punch the guy who just beat you in the four-hundred-meter dash—condition us to manage ourselves. Obeying the unwritten rules is a good thing for a young man's career, female relationships, and personal happiness prospects, as well as his success in the game.

The Code of the Sportsman

Being a "good sport" is one of those colloquial phrases we use without thinking much about what it means. A good sport is a person who knows how to follow rules, play hard, and be generous in victory and gracious in defeat.

Since professional sports has become an industry, these attitudes are getting harder to find. Value and support any coach who takes these values to heart—he or she is worth more to your son than a record-setting season.

Learning to Be Coachable

If you've ever tried to teach children a skill, you know what a valuable quality responsiveness to the input of an adult can be. And it doesn't matter if your son is the star player or a bench-rider. One benefit of sports is that sons who won't listen to parents' coaching will perk right up in the presence of another adult with the authority to decide his future on the team. Expose your son to this external input early and often. It's the sort of social pressure that brings more positive than negative.

Never Quit

One of the premier lessons of sports involvement is that you've got to finish what you begin. Don't let your son quit a sport or give up on himself midseason. Even if he doesn't like the coach or fellow players. Remember, this isn't supposed to be all fun. A little life lesson—learning is good. Push him. Better yet, help him push himself.

But here's an exception: Some coaches are truly idiotic. (Coaching may be the last bastion where truly rude and abusive behavior is sometimes accepted.) If your sensibility tells you a coach is unreasonably harsh or obsessed, talk with him or her about it. If you aren't convinced that having your son continue is a great idea, ask other parents and get some perspective. If you still come up negative, yank him. Fortunately, there are plenty of talented coaches around doing great things with kids.

A Little Pain Is OK

Nobody likes pain, but learning to handle it is a trademark of mature manhood. Young men must be tested to feel good about themselves. Tested through difficulty and trial—perhaps even some blood, broken bones, and tears. The point is that we need to help our sons become upstream-swimmers. And talk won't do it.

Put your son in competitive situations and let him become sparked with the desire to push himself. This spark often springs out of a desperate and mean experience—running wind sprints, playing defensive tackle, getting up at 5 A.M. for early practice.

Get out of the way. Your kid needs to hurt and play on anyway.

And Moms, let your son become a man.

Dads, take him to the brink of trouble and cut him loose. Life is his battle to fight, and your role is to build something enduring and tough in him, not to be a pack mule who will carry him there.

In Pursuit of the Dream

In conclusion, help your son find good role models in both sports and music. They exist, but they usually aren't the ones promoted by Madison Avenue. The stars who fill the sports magazines or are used to promote products are not used for their role-model value. They're chosen and groomed for their ability to attract attention—a pretty poor substitute for character.

Also, subscribe to periodicals that promote *action and participation* versus *voyeurism and consumerism*. Most reporting on music and sports these days caters to our impulse to gawk at people who we think are more significant than ourselves. But our kids are already chronic watchers. Find magazines that match your son's interests and actually help him *do* them.

As a final thought, remember—you are witnessing a miracle here. Your boy is growing into a man. What a wonderful thing to be part of! Your son's heart is expressing itself through the simplicity of music, the mystery of the arts, the pure physical exuberance of sports and recreation. This miracle is worthy of your attention and participation. Connect with something God is already doing: shaping your son's character strengths and lifelong passions.

Chapter Twelve

Hard Times
Can Create Heroes

Transforming adversity into growth

Not long ago I was the keynote speaker at a sobering event. It was a breakfast to honor twelve high school students in the area who had overcome adversity in some area of their lives. Despite their trials, these teenage men and women had pushed forward and endured, often in the face of tearjerking agony.

One quiet student sat next to me during the ceremony. He was a kid of seventeen, his face full of zits. You can guess my interest when I heard him accept his first-place scholarship. Among many atrocities, he'd been repeatedly beaten by his stepfather as a boy (and frequently hospitalized), shipped from pillar to post with the label of "incorrigible," and finally adopted by his grandparents, who believed in him and loved him.

What really got me was when the moderator of the event read what this kid said about his community: "I live in the best community in the world. I have the greatest grandparents anyone could ever have. My school has the best teachers and administrative staff in the entire state. I know I'm going to do well in my life because I live with the greatest people anywhere."

What makes a seventeen-year-old, pockmarked kid say things like this? No one knows why some kids endure hell on earth yet end up being role models while others with more advantages turn to drugs, crime, and bitterness.

How some kids learn how to respond to everyday adversities fascinates me. As a dad of teenage boys about to launch into an adversity-filled world, I think there's a powerful lesson lying hereabouts...

Life Hurts

Whether you live under a rock or in the world's grandest palace, one thing remains constant: Life brings disappointments, pain, and tragedies. And teenagers tend to see these adversities through 10X glasses. Their lives have an inescapable intensity that heightens every experience they have. As a result, even small things create hardship.

Adversity for teens could include:

- not making a sport
- rejection by a girl
- parents fighting
- making a mistake and getting caught
- a physical or mental handicap
- loss of a friend
- parents are getting divorced
- bad skin, shortness, or weight problems
- a move to a new school
- a really bad haircut
- no money for cool clothes

We all face adversity from the moment the morning alarm goes off to the last brain blip of the day. It's upstream, baby. No place for wimps. Life, it seems, is somehow woven with adversity. It's almost as if life can't happen without it.

Facing adversities seems easier when we hear stories of others who've faced the challenges and won. Thankfully, we find them throughout Scripture.

The Bible is a book about troubles—and people overcoming them. Adversity and tribulation dog almost every character in the Bible. Maybe that's why they're mentioned. If you want a road map for leading into and out of troubles, open the Bible and jump on the Interstate.

I've noticed an odd marriage between God and struggles. An oft-quoted line regarding adversity says, "If it doesn't kill you, it'll make you stronger." I've tested that aphorism, and it's true. God uses adversity for His own purposes (consider Hebrews 11–12). Our goal should not be to avoid adversity but to use it and learn from it.

That's not easy to do as adults. How do we lead our teenage men to make the best of something as unlikable as adversity?

A Parent's Dilemma

We have to deal with a fundamental conflict when it comes to our kids and adversity. Our job as parents is to equip our kids for real life—the good and the bad. We know this is our mission, and we know all the troubles life can dish out. But warring within us is our natural instinct to protect our kids from pain and suffering. Because we love our kids, we hate to see them encounter defeat or loss of any kind. Our instinct is to protect them from hardships if we can.

Both of these parental urges—to equip and to protect—are good.

And here's the good news: We can do both. In fact, by actively helping our kids cope with adversity in healthy, character-building ways, we are ultimately protecting them by helping them prepare for life's blows.

In other words, if you shield your son from life's rough edges, you'll handicap him for life. Remember the provocative-parenting rule: to change metaphors. Ultimately you "protect" your son when you allow him to sandpaper himself against life as he's growing up.

Ouch!

For some of you, that image might conjure up bleeding brush-burns and for others, a beautiful piece of finely finished furniture. Think furniture. Shielding can be fatal. You protect them best by sanding them now.

I've had to discipline myself to let adversity happen to those I love, then coach them through it. This has not been easy. Adversity, however, might be the key to making your son the best person he can possibly be.

A Closer Focus

Outright Blowup

When a young man loses his temper, it won't last forever; nor will the explosion solve much. In other words, after he settles down, you'll still be faced with something that needs fixing.

Don't focus on the event—what silly or hurtful thing he did or said. Focus your wisdom and patience instead on getting past the blowup and moving on to the job of repair. Let your son have some cool-down time. That may be as long as hours, but try not to let it go overnight. Then sit down across from him and tell him that you both have a problem that needs fixing, and you need his help to get anywhere.

Help in Hard Times

The next time your son encounters disappointment or pain, give him a hug and tell him you love him. Then look your son in the eye and try to help him remember some key points:

The world ain't really over. *The problem:* Teenage boys think that when their girlfriends dump them, the world is ending and they'll be miserable forever.

The principle: Remember that adversity for teenagers is life-and-death stuff. Much like a small boy doesn't know a small cut won't kill him, a big boy doesn't know that life's adversities won't ruin him. He needs to be taught that. He needs to experience survival firsthand. Without the guiding words of someone who's been there—you—he's going to flounder around in worry and grinding hopelessness. This is a dangerous place.

The plan: Try to help him get some perspective. Share a personal war story. Better yet, remind him of a past crisis he faced, now long forgotten. When I was practicing family counseling I often wondered whether the best value I served was simply to take people's eyes off their suffering long enough for time to heal. Time is a great medicine. Time is on your son's side, and he needs to discover that.

It's still up to you. *The problem:* When teens get victimized, they often give up.

The principle: When people feel they control the circumstances they're facing (whether or not they actually do), their chances of being successful skyrocket. When they lose hope, however, and believe they're helpless to influence their situation, they quit. Some people, because they've never learned how to effectively influence their own lives, learn to be helpless.

Apply this lesson to your teenager. Keep in mind that it really doesn't matter what kind of adversity your boy encounters. What really matters for healthy growth is that he feels as though he can do something about his adversity. He must perceive or feel that he has options available when trouble strikes. Young men who don't feel they have options become despondent and give up.

The plan: Help him see that he has options, power, and control. I'm a writing freak. Being visual, I like to write out my options on paper and look at them. I encourage kids facing struggles to do the same so they can see more options than they currently do. Listing them on a sheet jogs new ideas and helps them get a "feel" for what's actually in their personal arsenal. If your son does this, it will also allow you a peek inside his head, and best of all, it will allow you the chance to suggest new ideas and input. In short, it helps put a sense of control back where it belongs.

A small step is huge. *The problem:* Teens have trouble figuring out where to begin fixing something that goes wrong.

The principle: Teenage boys are notorious for wanting to fix their tribulations in one swift move. Once the trouble begins, their instinct is to take one jump and be done. They don't always understand that solving problems often takes time and many steps. As a result, they become despondent when the first thing they try fails to solve a mess.

This is complicated when life, at times, seems stacked with problems one after another. Fixing this tall stack of difficulties seems too much to handle. So they want to surrender.

The plan: Help your son take one step at a time. "You didn't make the starting team in basketball. So ask your coach what one skill he thinks you should focus on improving."

Encourage him to break down individual problems in short steps and to tackle his mounting difficulties one at a time. This won't come naturally to him, so you'll need to coax and encourage him to keep his focus on the next step—just the next step. At first, when he begins to do this, he'll discover that taking short steps does work to get out of messes. But his attention span won't hold this perspective for long. Internally, he's too hyper, and he'll drift from the slower, methodical wisdom he needs. Be patient and help him focus on just the next step.

Headfirst is smart. *The problem:* Teens struggle with the urge to run or avoid problems.

The principle: Heroes run toward trouble. Teach your son that the best course for handling trouble is head-on.

Hebrews admonishes us to, "Come boldly to the throne of grace, that we may obtain mercy and find grace to help in time of need" (4:16, NKJV). God likes to look at us face to face. He wants us to approach Him boldly, face first, especially in times of great trial. He wants us to look up and smile. This is not easy. It's learned.

This is not only a great lesson and insight into the heart of God, it's also a great life lesson. Help your son grasp the value of tackling life head-on. Look into the eyes of trouble, not over the shoulder at it from a dead run.

Recently I accompanied a group of teenagers to Chicago for some inner-city youth-mission work. Before we started working one day, we shared our fears with one another. The fears ran the gamut from gang encounters to having interaction with dirty, homeless people to hating bugs and rodents. Our prayer was that God would grant us eye-to-eye boldness. We promised to look for God to act on our "boldness before the throne of grace" and to report back that night what God did.

That evening was a time of jaw-dropping stories of God's faithfulness. God loves boldness. I witnessed it!

The plan: Show your son that it's better to face problems head-on. "Make an appointment with that teacher and ask him why he seems unwilling to help you understand," or "I don't know what you're going to do about your car payment, but what do you think would be the most effective course of action?"

Sometimes I sit down with my kids and actually show them a struggle or problem I'm having in my life and how I plan to address it. I've been pleasantly surprised to find they had no idea about the scope of problems actually on my plate and were very interested to know what I was going to do.

The swamp has a rainbow in it. *The problem:* Teenagers see only the bad, the difficult, the pain.

The principle: Help your son learn how to look for good in bad situations. "It's sad that we're moving. But could there be some good to come from getting to start over fresh at a new school? Hey, girls always check out the new guys. And nobody will tease you about that time you fell off the riser during your band concert."

The plan: Teach your son the 50/20 rule. Around our house everyone knows the 50/20 rule. It's taken from Genesis 50:20, where Joseph philosophizes about one of his life's worst adversities: being sold as a slave when he was a young boy.

Joseph was the favorite son of the Hebrew patriarch Jacob. His brothers, being intensely jealous, sold him to some camel traders heading toward Egypt. Many harrowing years later, Joseph, now the number-two guy in Egypt, was reunited with his brothers and got to visit his dad before he died.

But the brothers were certain that Joseph would have them killed after their dad died, so they scrambled to ask Joseph for forgiveness. To their total surprise, Joseph said, "As far as I'm concerned, God turned into good what you meant for evil. He brought me to the high position I have today so that I could save the lives of many people." He was a pretty cool Joe.

What can we learn (and teach) from this? God can and does take bad situations and use them for good. When we trust and believe the 50/20 rule in faith, we begin to see it happening all around us. It is one of the most exciting and faith-building observations I know of.

God wants to do this for you! He wants to do it for your son! Are you watching for it?

Hero-Making

It's important to help our kids cope with adversity. Hard times truly can build character and coping skills. But making heroes requires much more than that.

Remember the kids I mentioned at the beginning of this chapter? These kinds of heroes aren't simply teens who learned to cope with adversity. They are teens who are transformed by their hardships and who, in turn, will transform their world. Real heroes are heroes in the everyday world. What they do is simple and matter of fact. They do it without the benefit of a standing ovation. They usually don't die in the process. Heroism boils down to one person making a brave choice at a difficult time.

That's what we want for our kids. But few of us take the time to instill such heroic qualities in them.

I've read many stories of heroic deeds, selfless acts, and tremendous courage. As I've read those stories, the same questions go through my head: *Would I do that? Could I do that if faced with the same challenge? Would my kids do that?* And finally, *What can I do to prepare my kids to be that kind of person?*

We don't want to necessarily force kindness and goodness but action born of an inward desire. We cannot effectively create a hero by twisting a boy's earlobe. All we can do is plant the field and highlight the opportunities as often as possible.

But I've got some news: We won't fail for two reasons. First, the teenage years are the age of heroism, and second, teenage men, deep in their hearts, long for the opportunity to do something special.

Here are some heroic character qualities:

- service to others at cost to self
- courage in the face of fear
- unwavering determination in the face of failure
- great faith—a vision for eternal purposes

Like so many of God's great principles, these qualities tend to run counter to our natural responses. As parents, our job is simply to show our sons where and how to apply their efforts and to create opportunities where we can.

Can You Help Me? (service to others)

A hero is someone who is willing to go beyond the call of duty to help others. And he is willing to draw on whatever gifts, skills, and life experiences—especially his own adversities—to help. He is the twenty-year-old ex-addict who counsels teens on how to avoid the drug trap. He is the guy who always stays after a school performance to help his tired teacher take down the equipment.

Many young men respond to a direct, verbal request for heroism. Simply saying, "I need your help," has powerful repercussions. Uttering the words, "I need a hero," stirs something deep in every young man I've known.

"Team heroics" is another great way to teach teens heroism. Young men can learn heroism when they're following a hero. There's a carry-over effect. Let the cutting edge be you, and let your son join you in helping you do a heroic act as simple as holding doors for others in a

The Chore War

Unless your teenage son grew up on a farm, he is wired to think of household tasks as menial, unfair, punitive, boring, surely someone else's responsibility...you know the scene. (Kids raised on farms think that, too, but the relationship between working and eating is clear in the country. That helps.)

Our kids have grown up in a push-button world. Even the cut-along-the-dotted-line packaging on microwave dinners annoys them. But work is necessary for growing good men. Boring, hard, nasty work is even better—we learn more about life and ourselves from it. A daily to-do list of jobs requiring five to ten minutes' work, perhaps more on the weekends, seems reasonable.

If chores are new to your house, tackle them like any training (behavior modification) project:

- Get your son's attention from the start: "Sorry, things are changing."
- Create a chore list then let him choose which tasks he'll do.
- Describe clearly what "done" means.
- Describe awards for completion.
- Establish consequences for failure.

Chores aren't the only effort a child is responsible for. He expects food and shelter from you, and frankly, there's nothing wrong with your asking for help when you need it. Use the clock. Ask for ten, twenty, or thirty minutes of his time.

Play the "hero" card to keep down the complaining. (You're looking for a hero to do a hard project—no wimps or complainers, please.)

And chores needn't always be housework. How about grocery shopping, doing volunteer work, raking leaves for a neighbor, or writing Grandma a letter?

store, picking up litter for no reason, or helping a stranded motorist. The possibilities for team heroics are as varied as your daily life.

But as parents, we often miss the chances for everyday heroics. In my seminars I often highlight that by saying, "We are who we are most comfortable being." I mean that God has given us certain combinations of gifts and qualities. It's our job to adjust ourselves to be comfortable with those gifts and qualities and use them for His purposes. Too often our lives get taken over by the limiting patterns of our comforts rather than the patterns of our real abilities.

In Luke 12:48, Jesus said, "To whom much is given, from him much will be required" (NKJV). He didn't say those words to scare His disciples. He wanted to remind them of the power of the truth He was revealing and to call them to action.

Remind your son of his gifts often, and call him forward to use them.

Then let him know that you are certain he is destined for greatness. You'll fix in your son something explosive.

Brave Moves (courage in the face of fear)

A hero is not someone who is unafraid. A hero is someone who is afraid—yet faces what he fears. A great book called *Feel the Fear and Do It Anyway* by Susan Jeffers aptly describes this.

What do such "feel the fear" opportunities look like in a teen's life? Only rarely do they involve adrenaline-pumping challenges such as running into a burning building. Usually they have to do with his areas of weakness or insecurity. He's shy, but he's been asked to address the student council. Or maybe he's dying to ask a certain girl to the prom. He wants to try out for the swim team, but he's afraid he won't make it. He's afraid to tell you the truth about what happened Saturday night, but he makes the leap.

How do you encourage such choices to be brave? For starters, suggest to him that fear isn't bad. In fact, in some ways it's really great. Facing his fears *is* one of the most fulfilling things he can do.

Life is filled with what I call "destiny moments," those instances where something needs to be done and someone must act. We all encounter probably three or four every day. If I'm the one who steps forward, I feel great about it. If it ends up being someone else, I feel less than great and spend some time scolding myself.

Help your son search and seize his destiny moments.

Did You Say "Impossible"? (relentless determination)

I know some people for whom the concept of "impossible" literally does not exist. I'm attracted to these kinds of people. Once I was involved in a meeting where a Mafia-hit-man-turned-evangelist was attempting to establish a prison ministry in a local state penitentiary. The final word from the warden was simple: "This project will only go forward on orders directly from the governor, and you'll probably never get that."

A Closer Focus

Heroic Opportunity

Choose an area or topic where your son can rescue you: a computer task, understanding a *Rolling Stones* cover treatment, watching a sport on TV, playing a video game, or thinking through a local teen-related news story. Let your son know you're looking for a hero. Be genuine and persistent in your interest—and watch how differently he treats you. Consider how demoralizing it might be to live in a house where a parent considered himself or herself the "fount of all knowledge."

I was shocked. My reaction was, "Well, let's forget it. What's for lunch?"

The Mafia-man-turned-evangelist, however, was cut from a different cloth. He said, "OK, what's his name, and when can I see him?" It just so happened that we were meeting near the state capital. So what did this hit man/evangelist do? Our small entourage followed Mr. No-Impossibility directly to the state capital. We marched up to the governor's office and simply asked to see the big guy. Well, we didn't get to see the governor that day, but the evangelist set an appointment for the following week, secured his permission to start the program—and runs it throughout the state to this day.

He had no idea what *impossible* meant. Seeing it firsthand like that did something to me. I started ignoring impossibility too.

If your teen would adopt this kind of thinking, imagine the possibilities: "Admission into a *great* college? Where do I get the application?" or "Actually run for city council at eighteen? Where do I sign up?" or "Share my beliefs with someone who is totally antagonistic? I can do that."

In Mark 2, Jesus was preaching in a home. The place was packed. Standing outside were several men waiting with their crippled friend, knowing that if they could just get inside, Jesus would heal him.

Many of us would have walked away from that adversity, certain there was nothing more we could do. But these men were true heroes. They climbed onto the roof of the house, cut a hole, and lowered their buddy down right in front of Jesus.

Heaven in Mind (great faith and vision for eternal purposes)

At its root, heroism is the result of faith. A hero has faith that is based on an eternal, greater purpose. I can't help but think of young David, probably a teenager, taking on Goliath. He sought no personal glory. He just wanted to serve God and protect his people. Simple desire birthed great action. This compelling story is a lesson showing how simple devotion to God leads to a tremendous upswing in action.

In Hebrews 11:1, the author wrote, "Faith is the substance of things hoped for, the evidence of things not seen" (NKJV). Then in the rest of the chapter he rolls out his hall of fame: Abel, Enoch, Noah, Abraham and Sarah, Isaac, Jacob, Joseph, Moses and his parents, Joshua, Rahab, and others. These are men and women who, at the height of difficulty and danger, changed history through self-sacrifice, courage, and determination—and simple devotion to something heavenly.

Heroism and faith go together. To be a man of faith is an act of great heroism, and to be a hero is an act of great faith. God has a way of blessing young men who are willing to do both.

As parents, we are invited to look deep into our teenage son's inner being and recognize a greater possibility than anything others might have noticed or anything he has proved or anything he has even indicated wanting—and know beyond a doubt that it is true.

The evidence of a hero in the making...

Trouble? Come what may...

PART FOUR

_____

SHAPING A MAN'S SOUL

Chapter Thirteen

Celebrating the Passage

Helping your son make the "rite" move

My path through the land of teen-building often leads to unusual places. The Red Cliff Ascent is one of those places. It's a ranch for wayward young men in Utah, an Outward Bound kind of program.

Ranches like the Red Cliff Ascent are the treatment facilities of last resort for hard-core teenagers. The primary therapeutic tool they use is to subject young men to measured physical challenges in order to build their sense of achievement, skill, teamwork, respect, and maturity.

The theory is simple: Put young men in positions of moderate physical deprivation, palpable danger, and extreme fear to test their limits and help them discover resources they didn't previously know they had. It pits hardheaded young men against a mother they can't manipulate—nature. This therapy has rescued many boys stranded on the shoals of manhood.

Why do we need programs like this? Because they give young men something badly needed: achievement they can touch, review, and brag about. Let's face it, a hundred years ago probably no one thought that climbing rocks in predictable panic could lead anyone to manhood. But a hundred years ago they didn't have a society that discouraged young men from character-building activity.

All young men need to be put to the test—not just to test what they can do but to test who they are at their very core. Only then can they start to act and think like winners.

Why Is This Such a Big Deal?

A boy's ascent to manhood is a twisting, uncertain journey. It involves other adults and highly personal challenges from him. In the past we've called this natural process *feeling his oats, rites of passage,* and *coming of age.* It's a vital transition that gets lost or muddied in an MTV world.

But how many boys of our own generation went through some rite of passage? Probably none of them did—at least, no ritual more trying than getting a hickey, a driver's license, or a hangover. So why should we require something of the next generation that we and others before us did fine without?

Life goes on, and boys are tough. They'll survive with or without rites of passage. We can let them slide into life unsure and weak. But if we have an opportunity to use a teenage boy's need for meaningful rites of passage to make a strong impact, should we? Yes. We should seize anything that might help make him extraordinary.

The Babble Zone

In dealing with this topic of transition to manhood, we're entering a zone of psycho/politico/feminist babble. Many people want to correct the "problem" with men in general, though they're often deeply divided on what they believe men ought to be. Many hotly debated ideologies have arisen over what boys and men should be, how they should be it, and when.

But boys are boys. And boys are often crude, mean, rough, unpolished, and unpredictable. They cleanly slip out of the social clothing we expect them to wear with a smile. No amount of psychological theory, legal initiative, or feminist wishes will change it.

My purpose in this chapter is not to condone the behavior of these young savages but to shed light on it so as to build great men. I want to give you a practical and sensible way of handling boy-to-man transitions. I'm certain our friends at the Red Cliff Ascent wouldn't mind fewer guys needing to be fixed.

Making Sure We Take the Right Rite

Several years ago, rites of passage were used as a means of ushering young men into manhood. These included ancient cultural observances like bar mitzvahs among the Jews, the "Walkabout" among Australian aborigines, and various ceremonial rituals by Native Americans. Today, however, that simple, basically harmless idea has gotten mixed up with a mishmash of psychology and mythology.

Let's back up. What is a rite? A rite is an outward acknowledgment or demonstration of an inward reality. As a symbol of "passing" the outward demonstration, young men normally acquire an outward symbol of manhood: a bone through the nose, a tattoo, or maybe a Yamaha motocross bike, depending on the culture. These symbols are given in expectation that something has *really* changed inside.

Should Christian parents care about passage-making for their sons? Does the Bible shed any light on the subject?

Yes. In Proverbs we see Solomon, one of the wisest men of all time, passing along life wisdom to his sons so they would properly align themselves with God. Specifically, he wrote this advice "for attaining wisdom,...for acquiring a disciplined and prudent life,...for giving prudence to the simple,...for understanding proverbs and parables, the sayings and riddles of the wise" (Proverbs 1:2-4,6). In short, for creating inner change.

At the time, proverbs were used by parents and teachers to impart wisdom in a way that was challenging. One theme running throughout the book of Proverbs is the idea of "skillful living," skill being synonymous with wisdom and living in a God-honoring way.

Sounds like a rite to me—and a test worth trying to pass.

Let's boil this discussion down to a list of propositions:

- Young men need to test themselves—against themselves and against stronger, older men.
- Older guys understand this intuitively; women don't.
- Young men need to win.
- Older men must make younger men earn the win, not give it.
- Emotions can run high and hot during this period.
- Only after making his passage is a boy a man, ready to carry his weight and contribute his part in the family and the community.

Gladiators in Ball Caps

Within every boy is an indelible desire to prove himself to himself. I know, I know: A boy has value "just because," and he should know it. But he doesn't know it. He wants to prove his value over and over. And that will never change, no matter how many self-esteem classes he attends. He will constantly try to prove his worth until he's proven himself to himself. It's not unlike the gladiators of yore.

This can get nasty. Ask your boy which "law" rules his school: the golden rule or the law of the jungle. After he finishes yodeling like Tarzan, ask for some specific examples and brace yourself.

The competitive law of the jungle is the reality of an adolescent boy's life. Social life is a boy-eat-boy, big-dogs-run-in-front game. It's not fun, especially if you're near the bottom of the food chain. Animals instinctively prepare their offspring for this kind of life via hard experiences. They make the youngsters fight their way up the pecking order, kill rivals, and help them dominate their peers, if they can.

Rather than eating the competition, we humans expect our boys to play hard, sweat lots, and beat out the rivals. But our boys would engage in competitive adventures by themselves even if we weren't around! Without strong, cool-headed adults around, boys would probably kill each other to prove themselves. (Maybe that's why William Golding's *Lord of the Flies* is required reading in most high schools.) If you doubt this, pick up a newspaper and read what kids are doing to each other in our inner cities. It would be nice if a boy could find manhood through weekend retreats, but for most teens the real proving ground is a back alley. Boys know they'll never find big-dog status reading poems or getting in touch with their feelings.

A Closer Focus

The Need for Speed

A rite of passage for boys always involves taking the family car out and seeing what it'll do. Wide open. In his mind, he's Mario Andretti. But *you* know he's just Morry in a minivan. This spells trouble.

Make it clear that he's not to race the car (see "The Car Deal," chapter 6). Spread the word among adults in your town that you want to know if they see your minivan hot-rodding around town. Parents talking about what they see is a great way to make the kids safe, the roads safe, and save your sanity.

Competition Is Key

To prove themselves, boys compete over anything: physical size, speed, scars, brains, homes, hair, girls, and six-pack abs. To an adolescent young man, competition is a means to personal qualification. They think, *If I can just win at something, I'll be able to look in the mirror and conclude I'm OK.*

So boys grow into men through competition.

- First, they test themselves against themselves.
- Then they test themselves against older men.

For example, when boys are younger they "pretend challenge" their dads. It can be a playful thing, like kidding around about being a tough guy or a macho man. But as puberty approaches, the challenges move from innocuous to serious, from occasional to almost constant.

Then suddenly, almost without warning, the challenge goes "live." The challenge is real, not playful. Ideally, nobody gets hurt. Almost all fathers can point to moments when the challenge went "live." It can be a difficult, intense moment that might feel to both parties like hatred and anger when it's really only a test. It's the son's first attempt to make his ascent.

This has happened to me on several occasions with my own sons and with other boys I've spent time with. I kid around a lot. In some instances, that flippancy has blinded me to the graveness these young men feel as they make their challenge. I know now that with teenage young men I can kid around too much. To some extent, they need a firm, mature resistance against which they can hurl themselves for the test.

On the surface, the young guys get uppity and smart, acting macho and flexing themselves. Below the surface, they want to be all right, but they don't know what all right is. They're groping for ways to feel adequate and strong.

The Image of Success vs. the Real Thing

We live in a perception-driven society. We want to look a certain way, regardless of how we feel under the surface. Businessmen want to wear the right tie, businesswomen want the right attaché. Unfortunately, if we're weak and depleted under the surface, our inadequacies won't wait long to show themselves.

As young men mature, they begin to feel a clawing emptiness inside. Not knowing quite what it is, they attempt to remedy it by adopting certain postures and images. They might throw themselves completely into an identity. One boy is into soccer. Another, often in the same family, is into odd music. Another wears Tommy Hilfiger. When these identities don't help (and they all exhaust themselves), anxieties rise like a bad temperature. This self-preoccupation can lead to an irrational need to win or be on top. It's bad chemistry for happiness.

What was Satan's sin, the one that got him booted from the top seat? According to Isaiah, Satan was escorted to the door for one thing: vanity and an insatiable taste for more.

We must help our sons experience real achievement, not just empty symbols like clothing, tattoos, patches, earrings, or cars. Let's give them tangible experiences of real achievement and inner fulfillment.

How? Empty competitions are all take, take, take. But meaningful accomplishments happen when young men give and take in equal measure. Satisfaction comes with achieving a lasting sense of goodness rather than in collecting hollow symbols of it. It's only through maturity that young men learn to replace all the measuring and comparing of youth with the giving and taking of fruitful adulthood.

I once worked with a young man who was an Olympic-caliber figure skater. He was an ice dancer, and his laser intensity had burned out several partners. He couldn't see that his need to win was consuming the very partners he needed to secure the Olympic medal he dreamed about. Several coaches had discarded him as unteachable, and his career seemed destined for mediocrity.

A Closer Focus

Up in Smoke

When your son experiments with cigarettes and other tobacco products, you'll probably never know about it. But what if he goes further and begins casual usage or a habit?

Without question, cigarettes are a gateway drug to pot, crack, cocaine, LSD, and heroin. In addition, they're highly addictive and made that way on purpose. Nobody would smoke on his own. Our bodies have built-in mechanisms that make the experience difficult to enjoy. You have to *make* yourself enjoy it. And a fair number of teenagers do.

To influence this, we must appeal to our sons' self-interest, pointing out that smoking ruins your looks, makes your breath stink, makes breathing difficult, occupies your time hiding and planning, and is very expensive. If you want to stand out and be different and cool, you can find other options that work better.

If they smoke or hang out with smokers, set clear boundaries: This is not to be done by anyone in our cars, in our house, or on our property, not in the presence of any family member. Then concentrate on influencing that attitude about the behavior. You can't put out every cigarette, but you can usually douse a lifelong, health-threatening habit.

His problem was simply a lack of maturity. He needed to learn that rather than sucking the life out of his partners for his own one-sided aims, he needed to learn to give back. He needed to be shown that he could be even more competitive if he simply cared about his partner's aspirations, challenges, and successes as well as his own. Young men learn this only through the input of adults, especially the input of older men. With help, this young skater went on to become the national champion and Olympian he aspired to be.

And what's more, he became a better man.

Making an Event—An Invitation from Dad

Moms and dads play different key roles in helping this passage make sense to their sons. First, let me talk about the role Dad plays.

The point of creating an event is to make him aware of the need to step up to manhood. There is no exact right or wrong way to do this. What is crucial is that your invitation to conduct the challenge be personal and somewhat serious, that the test be taxing, and that your affirmations of his success be genuine. Remember, you are giving your son the birthright of manhood, the right to feel that he belongs with adult men and can exist on a par with them.

All you really want is for your son to be able to look in the mirror and say, "I am a man."

That's inner realization. To accomplish this, some dads give their boys clear assignments. For example:

- *A mental assignment:* Have your son read something, write down some life goals, fill in his family tree, or interview an older relative.

- *A physical assignment:* Invite him to accomplish something that has special meaning for the family or for himself, like climb a mountain, swim a lake, or camp overnight alone somewhere.

- *A spiritual assignment:* Ask him to memorize key life verses from the Bible or write a prayer for his life.

- *A celebration assignment:* Invite him to participate in some kind of wing-ding with you or with another dad-son pair. This can be a good time to talk about sexuality, family priorities, reminiscing on your son's life story, owning up to difficult facts or failures. It's an opportunity to sit around the fire (or Three Rivers Stadium) with "the guys."

Passage-Making on Ordinary Days

In addition to one-time ceremonies and events, invite your son into manhood all through his adolescence. Some young men are more influenced by daily challenges that help prove themselves to themselves. You still need to tell your boy he qualifies, but look for daily opportunities for him to discover it internally.

One problem with this is that your emotions and his run abnormally high throughout this whole period. His challenges and childish "put up your dukes" antics can be exasperating. Like many dads, you might find yourself saying or doing dumb things in response that effectively strip him of the manhood you want desperately to give him. How do you deal with this?

I'll never forget the day I asked my elder son, Jake, about a personal matter I'd overheard him discussing on the phone. I don't normally listen in on his conversations, so I was as innocent and inquisitive as I knew how to be. His reply was terse and clear: "My private life is none of your business."

I choked. I remembered when he was a little boy and how we'd romp and play and go camping and enjoy our special times together—all so this moment would never happen! But here was my deepest fear, staring back at me.

I replied badly. "What do you mean, your private life is none of my business? Who do you think you are, you little punk?" It was a memorable exchange. It's amazing our kids grow up sane.

I suppose we men never outgrow our competitive nature. By the grace of God—and much forgiveness from our boys—we can mellow and become patient and kind. By the grace of God we can all learn and grow and depend on one another rather than bicker and fight and contend our way through these precious and defining moments of our boys' lives.

A Dad's Guide to Peaceful Passages

Here are some suggestions for removing the fight and the competition during the slow transition to manhood:

Maintain a list of what you do well. You need to be secure in who you are and where your talents lie, because your son will test your strength. Without knowing your own strengths and feeling confident in them, you might crumble.

Think up five strengths and write them down. Within the next twenty-four hours you're going to need a boost. Your boy intends on winning his challenges with you. By definition that means you lose. It stings, and unless you're grounded in what you know are your granite strengths, you'll likely retaliate with a bite. We all have a lot of boy left in us! Let's rise above that.

If you can't think of five things you do well, ask your wife or friends. Chances are reasonably good that they know you better than you know yourself.

Learn how to fight gently. Remember when you were a kid? Competitions, whether verbal or physical, were games of force. You won by being more forceful with your wits, strength, or emotions. You learned that lesson so well that you still use it today. Often to your detriment.

There are three ways to reply to your son's challenges. One is to challenge back and make him "beat you." Another is to ignore his challenges completely. I believe that competing with Dad is vital and ignoring the challenge is actually rude. So I suggest you not ignore his challenges. However, I see no growth-enhancing value in crushing him with your power and force either. Some in-between third choice seems more reasonable.

When your son challenges you, reply in measured force, no matter how big or small the challenge. For example, you might let your son beat you in a close wrestling match. Allow him to make a great point of logic in a difference of opinion. (When discussing differences of opinion, too many dads inadvertently strip manhood off their sons like bark off a tree.) Or let your son offer constructive criticism on the way you're dressed (without a snide comeback).

Learn to struggle publicly a bit. Call it the "Forrest Gump Rule." Like Forrest Gump, exposing your weaknesses in plain, open innocence can summon a calming and helping response from your son. Expose your imperfections, assuming you have some!

Early in their lives, boys believe the adults around them are angels. They believe it because that's what we usually communicate to them. With the arrival of adolescence, however, boys gain the ability to sift through all the hype we use to promote ourselves and our spotlessness.

To some extent your son will believe you are a phony and a liar if you fail to 'fess up to your own imperfections. You're no angel, and the quicker you put that on the table, the more swiftly your relationship will grow.

Will you lose credibility? Ask Forrest Gump. Not only will you gain credibility, but you'll also gain a reason to be liked and assisted. That's power.

Ask your son to teach you something or be your encourager in a key area. Your son knows how to do things you don't. Perhaps it's sports related or artistic or craft or music related. Asking him to teach you provides a rare chance for him to be the expert. He'll be delighted to give, and that's a delight you don't want to miss.

Your son wants to connect with you, but the jungle of rules, power struggles, and past history combine to make connecting a struggle. Inviting him to teach you things bypasses all these troubles. And asking him to teach you something satisfies the need motivating all the competition: The need to be good at something and know it matters!

Try to be a good student. This means being wide-eyed and eager. Avoid complaining and asking questions you know he can't answer. And by all means, do your homework! When my sons try to teach me something, I give extra effort to learning it well so I can show them what a great job they did.

This happened once when I was trying to learn scales on a viola. My son Jake showed me a simple scale, and though I looked physically impaired and sounded worse, I worked and worked at it. Then about a week later, I pulled out the viola and played the scale perfectly. Naturally he told me how I could be even better. Now we're getting somewhere!

A Closer Focus

Scouting for Talent

Ask your son to tell you the things he does particularly well. Ask him to tell you what single thing he does best. Ask him to help you learn one thing on his list.

Ask your son to encourage you in something—being consistent in your quiet times or sticking with an exercise program. Boys don't live in a very encouraging world. They may not have any idea how to encourage us. And most don't yet understand that encouraging someone else can make them people of greater influence and confidence.

You may have to give your son the words to say—simple things like, "Hey, you can do it!" or "C'mon now, everything's gonna be all right." Asking him to be an encourager for you utilizes your son's desire to help and stand out. He'll feel good about it.

Put yourself on a praise schedule. You probably praise your son much less than you think. I make a predated list of things I will say to my sons: "Attaboy," or "You're really growing up so beautifully," or "You're one hot-shot kid," etc. And I make a list of things I'll do: give cards with one thing I really like about them, surprise them with a written invitation to do something they love, put gas in their cars.

Keeping a list helps me because I tend to get busy and overlook the little things that loom large in my sons' lives. And it helps me to direct my energies and defuse tensions that could squirt out in unhelpful ways.

The Rites of Mothers

As a mom, you bring a sense of emotional balance to your son and provide what may be for him the best possible interpretation of what effective masculinity is. Your words of encouragement and support have powerful influence on how he defines himself forever. Be a living affirmation of his value as a young man to you, and show him the pride you feel in seeing him grow.

Remember, boys want to be men, and they want to be good men.

As a mother, you may be in a better position to judge or articulate what that is more than any man alive. In some respects, you may be the most vital person to bring out the man in your son. Seize that position. He won't forget it.

As a mother, your son will always be your boy. He'll always have a special place in your heart, and you'll protect him to the death. At some point, that protectiveness can become overprotectiveness. Don't feel too bad about that. It happens to all mothers. Yet no matter how much you protect him, at some point you know he has to pull away from you and stand on his own. You might even point out men such as his father who demonstrate what standing alone is all about. The issue becomes complicated, however, when no man is around.

That's fine if the man you use to illustrate this is the boy's father, your husband. The issue becomes complicated, however, when no man is around. I'm frequently asked about situations where a single mom has no men available for this job. Or worse, the only men around are jerks.

If most of the men in your life are jerks, don't let that deter you from trying to put your son into the presence of a healthy, balanced man. Use your instincts. You'll know the difference, and though it's not always easy to arrange "unnatural" unions, even minimal contact can yield fruit. Look for tutors, coaches, youth-group leaders, bosses, uncles, or his best friend's dad. And be sure that you're not standing in the way of your son's relationship with his birth father.

If possible, encourage the man—or men—in your life to make themselves students of your son for a while. Ask for their wisdom, input, and help. Ask for a "consultation." Men are flattered to be approached for a job like this. They know what it means to be entrusted.

If you just can't find a healthy man, take heart. God places everyone in different circumstances for different reasons. It is neither random nor arbitrary. There are reasons. Sometimes the job of a seasoned believer is to seek God's purpose rather than to fight without faith. God has made our kids tough and resilient.

Making His Ascent

Rites of passage are about helping your son become a man who feels he can both belong and effectively take his place among men. Life just seems to work better when you feel as though you belong. You don't necessarily need pageantry and drama to mark this passage. But as parents we have many opportunities to point out the trail to the summit.

One of the miracles of growing up is that even in bad and unpleasant circumstances, boys can and do ascend to manhood. Without ritual, without a parent, without a clear plan—extraordinary young men still arrive! I'm not giving you an invitation to do nothing; I'm encouraging you to do everything with the strength that comes from quietness and confidence (see Isaiah 30:15).

God is always at work—isn't that the wonder of all the redemption stories going on everywhere around us? In this area of passage-making, I always encourage parents to be thankful for these mysterious paradoxes: Nothing is absolutely vital. Nor is anything absolutely toxic. Good parents make all the difference. Good kids survive lousy parents.

We can move forward to the best of our ability, ever vigilant and wide-eyed for opportunities that will serve our sons. But when all else appears to fail, we can know that God's hand always remains on our teenage men.

Our Father Himself is deeply involved in all the passages of man-making.

Chapter Fourteen

Laying a Foundation of Faith

His spiritual life is his ultimate destiny

The teen years are a time of reappraisal. Nothing in a teenager's mind is set in stone. No idea is permanent. No ideology beyond scrutiny. Everything is questioned. Nothing is sacred.

This worries us parents to death. Throughout most of our sons' childhoods we're lulled into a sense of safety by their relative compliance and wide-eyed belief in the sanctity of all we say. Then comes adolescence! No sooner do we think we've got the kids on the straight and narrow than they start asking some very prickly questions, refuse to go to church, think the Bible or the preacher is boring, dislike the Christian crowd at school…

These things are completely normal and nothing to get too ruffled about. It's common that after several years of questioning everything they've been taught—including the spiritual stuff—they will return more or less to what they learned as young boys. Whatever was laid down early in life leaves an indelible track that is easy to follow back. As Solomon said, "Train up a child in the way he should go, and when he is old he will not depart from it" (Proverbs 22:6, NKJV).

I encourage you to spend time developing a spiritual home base that your boy understands and can take with him through life. We're trying to build extraordinary boys here. That requires attention to a few details, and faith is one of the most promising ones. Let's look at some guidelines for this base building.

Keep Your Eye on the Big Prize

Consider Mary and Joseph. Any parent would be mighty proud to have a kid like Jesus. The short report we find in Luke 2:52 is one of the few glimpses we get of what Jesus was like as a teenager and a young man—"So Jesus grew both in height and in wisdom, and he was loved by God and by all who knew him" (NLT). It seems like precious few words to summarize such a long stretch of time, but maybe there's a lesson here.

Perhaps there are larger issues at stake with your teenager than how good a parent you are, his identity crisis, car insurance rates, or peer influences. Maybe one of those lessons is that we should keep our focus on something larger and more vital, something that places these niggling little details of raising great teenagers in their proper perspective.

No matter what you do, your kids eventually must make their own choices about God—who He is and what He wants. We cannot decide for them. It's a personal matter. We cannot twist them into a relationship with God. But we can let them know there is a bigger picture that matters eternally.

We don't have to be seminarians to accomplish this either. Did you read all the early church fathers or any German theologians before you came to faith? The gospel is simple. The kingdom of God is custom-made for kids.

And our faith looks a little crazy—just the kind of thing a provocative parent can relish.

Our Crazy Faith

Paul said our faith looks foolish to some people. Perhaps that includes your son. From the onset of early adolescence, boys almost instinctively begin to develop a spiritual sensitivity. Though they may have difficulty expressing the odd yearning, they sense a hollowness that begs to be filled.

Most people will ask penetrating questions in order to fill that hollowness. For Christians and those considering following Christ, the questions are predictable: "How can we believe the Bible?" "Was Jesus really perfect?" "How can we be certain He rose from the dead?" In some respects these questions are perfectly understandable. Radical faith is required to believe Jesus' claims, because they're amazing.

When trying to find good "filler" for their hollowness, teens pick the easiest options first. Following Jesus appears to be torturous and tough compared with worshiping nature, Buddha, MTV, or pizza. In comparison, Jesus seems demanding and difficult. Why would anyone volunteer for something so difficult? Well, they wouldn't, which is the reason many teenage boys opt for other things first.

But those other fillers eventually display their weaknesses. They have little substance or depth and provide only momentary satisfaction. Then the hunt for fulfillment continues. In the end, faith in Christ is more substantial than any of the other options.

Caution: The Guy Factor

In the survey I conducted of teenagers for this book, I asked two questions about God and religion. On both questions, the boys in the sample scored significantly lower than the girls. Their relatively negative attitudes about God and religion say something about them.

In chapter 2, I discussed the nature of evolving adolescent brains. For the first time they begin to see abstractions and shades of truth. And they are preoccupied with how they look to others, driven by pleasure/pain, peer dependent, distractible, and extremely competitive.

In light of this, I think boys often view God with some amount of disdain and mistrust—and any religion as weakness. The teen years are not the most receptive moments in a guy's life to risk a lifestyle he considers out of the norm or costly to his ego. The threat of public humiliation is just too much.

Another inhibition to spiritual responsiveness for our young men is that we are promoting it. Teenage boys have a certain allergy to our ideas. They aren't bad boys; they just turn west when we say east. They do this no matter how good and sensible your advice happens to be.

To worsen matters, some of our parental attitudes surrounding our faith do great damage. For example, we may subtly transmit a hostile mentality of: We're right and the rest of the world is not! That makes Christianity look small, territorial, and mean. Or we can hit the noes

A Closer Focus

Full Faith Workout

Take a step to place your faith outside your comfort zone and proceed toward it. In other words, don't fit God into your day; fit your day around God. For example, this weekend get up before dawn and go for a walk alone to pray. Pray about your young disciples. Jesus did. You'll be allowing your faith to change you, and you'll see your son from a fresh perspective.

and woes so hard that our teens never catch sight of the yeses and wows! If this is our overall attitude, we can grin and talk kindness all day, but our faith will appear uninviting and phony to our sons, and we will be slowly butchering our chances to touch them.

But we can do better. And fortunately, our young men are wired—whether they know it or will admit it—for a personal relationship with God. He has made sure of that. As spiritual tutors and mentors, parents have a lot to work with.

Building a Spiritual Home Base

We were created for personal connections—family commitments, sibling relationships, courting arrangements, and marriage. Your son is only beginning to discover the truth of his need. Another connection—a relationship with Jesus—will be the personal link between his true self and his most satisfying future. How do we encourage this connection?

Given the right atmosphere, the right foundation, every teenage boy can fill his need for connection with a personal relationship to the God of the universe. But since this is a private choice our sons must make, I suggest that we make good use of the provocative parenting rule, Don't force change; provoke it. Here are some provoking steps you can take.

Don't Get Religious; Get Happy

Any presentation of the gospel that does not include the element of happiness and peace is missing the point. Our faith is supposed to bring joy and happiness! It's supposed to make us smile and make us happy! Several years ago, I read a book by Tony Campolo called *The Kingdom of God Is a Party!* In that book, Campolo says that our salvation through grace is one of the happiest things a human being can experience. It's reason enough to tap your toes and wiggle your heart around a bit. Shouting and clapping wouldn't be entirely silly either. In fact, our salvation creates such deep, lasting joy that screaming and crying and dancing would be totally sensible.

So do it! Not for the sake of being a party animal but for the purpose of living, laughing, and loving. Jesus didn't go through death and resurrection to make you a sourpuss! Lighten up! Your kids will be more deeply moved by your own happiness than your pursed lips.

How do you normally persuade your teen? Do you lure him to your position or jam him into it? Yelling and harping at teenage boys is counterproductive. Proverbs 20:5 says, "Though good advice lies deep within a person's heart, the wise will draw it out" (NLT). Cornering teens and using pressurized, slam-jam techniques will result only in bitterness. Instead, find ways to present Jesus that gives the Spirit the greatest opportunity to let joy and celebration do their work.

Create Proximity

I was eight years old, listening to Billy Graham, when I made my decision to follow Christ. I was watching television alone, and Billy Graham told Jesus' parable of the prodigal son. I felt a tug and wanted to respond. When Billy made the path of invitation so clear, I decided to walk it. Accepting Christ was the right thing to do for me. And I thank my folks to this day for putting me in proximity to Billy Graham.

Find out where Christ is alive, and arrange for your son to be there. Look for speakers, athletes, missionaries, youth specialists, or anyone who is living life on the edge, especially those who are meaningfully involved in church. Look for people who make seeking Christ a joyful priority. And pursue meaningful relationships with other Christian family members and friends.

Elevate a church involvement above the level of movies or sleeping in late or other "take it as you feel it" options. Make it a matter of family commitment and passion.

Be Jesus Flavored

How do we position Jesus powerfully in our homes? Listen, even during these years when church is boring and religion is suspect to our boys, the person of Jesus is highly attractive. Jesus is someone they can touch. His radical rules and explosive encounters with the status quo have an immediate impact on a young man. Jesus is real, surprising, and down to earth.

Point your teen toward the accounts of Jesus' life and teachings in the Gospels. (He'll enjoy arguing his way through the Sermon on the Mount or the parables.)

And make Jesus attractive by being attractive yourself. Being like Jesus is the seasoning that will capture your son's taste buds. You begin to taste that way by emulating Jesus. Use His words. Memorize them carefully. Ask His questions. Give His responses. Say what Jesus might say in times of anger, excitement, confusion, anticipation, danger, or parties. Go away and pray alone a lot. There are examples of all these circumstances in the Bible.

Live with the same kind of radical faith and kindness He lived by. If you do, Jesus will becomes an actual, personal presence in your son's life. Represent for your son a relationship with God he can't fathom living without.

Get Excited about God's Word

It's not everyday that you get to hear God talk. Or is it? The Holy Bible is the wellspring of practically everything we know about God. A lot of it is transcription. Think about that. Do you demonstrate a thrill, a child-like fascination and effervescence about it? Your son will only be able to model what you show, so be thoughtful about how you present the Bible in your home. Get excited.

Help your son find entry points to the Bible with some pointers on where to start and how to make it part of his day. Help him make use of the tremendous resources for teen reading and inspiration available at your local Christian bookstore.

Get Caught in the Act (of giving your life away)

Following Christ is about giving: giving yourself, your time, your life. Not a real marketable ideology in contemporary America. Yet one of the greatest witnesses we can provide to our sons is unbridled, cheerful giving. Not just money either. Find things to give—time, compliments, candy, gifts, even blessings—and offer them with pleasure.

What seems to me to be an immutable law of the heart is that you really can't appreciate having something until you can appreciate giving it away. Giving something away without regard for what comes back is one of the highest human achievements. It's something we learn.

How do you learn it? By doing. Giving to those in need is a great way to help your son express his adventurous, idealistic side. A great example of this is when youth groups return from mission fields in Third World cultures. The attitude-changes that accompany these trips can be stunning. Suddenly the label on your pants means less when you meet people who have no pants.

Don't hesitate for a second to expose your kids to tough realities. If overseas trips aren't feasible, consider these possibilities: helping out at a senior care center, tutoring disadvantaged kids, working in a soup kitchen, or taking on a child sponsorship through an aid organization.

And remember the spiritual power of daily gratefulness. Lead forth-rightly in simple things like:

- giving thanks before meals
- saying thanks for favors
- expressing gratitude for everyday conveniences and kindnesses
- taking good care of the possessions you already own
- pointing out the need for your teens to do the same

Demonstrate the Joy of Imperfection

Teenagers think we expect perfection of them. They erroneously believe they must be perfect, and they know they're not! This convinces many of them that God wouldn't want anything to do with them, when exactly the opposite is true.

Our message needs to be clear and constant: Don't even try to be perfect! It's impossible, and it's not even the point!

A Closer Focus

Who Are You Becoming?

We must all remember that God is not nearly as interested in who we are as who we are becoming. Can we begin to think in a similar way about our boys?

One great exercise in faith and vision is to begin listing the kinds of "gifts" God has bestowed on our boys. Referring to this list can be a confidence builder for us, especially when our sons dis-appoint or surprise us in a negative way. We need a system in place to remind us where God is taking our sons, and this list serves the purpose well.

Take the time to start that list now, and keep it close at hand over the next few years.

In Matthew 9, Jesus was partying with an assortment of scum. Sinners really seemed to like Him. Several of Jesus' critics thought His social cavorting unseemly and told Him so. His words to them were direct and terse: "Now go and learn the meaning of this Scripture: 'I want you to be merciful; I don't want your sacrifices' [quoting Hosea 6:6]. For I have come to call sinners, not those who think they are already good enough" (9:13 NLT). With that He disappeared into Matthew's house.

Was Jesus clear enough? His point was aimed directly at the Pharisees' inner attitude about what He was doing here on earth. He didn't come to hang people by their spiritual thumbs for their imperfections. He didn't come as a grim reaper either. He came as a rescuer. A merciful rescuer. Certainly His challenge to us is to follow His example with our sons.

Drop Everything and Follow the Lead of the Spirit

In the book *Experiencing God*, authors Henry T. Blackaby and Claude V. King suggest that when the Spirit of God moves, we should cancel all our plans and follow. I try to practice this regularly, especially with my kids. God moves on them in crazy ways, and I try to be vigilant and sensitive in discerning when those moves are underway.

There is one very specific move of the Spirit you should sensitively pursue. Proclaiming verbally that Jesus is Lord is a vital step in accepting Christ. A public, open confession. Ask your son for this sort of proclamation if he hasn't done so already. When should you ask? When God opens the window. Not a minute sooner, not a minute later. Be sensitive and ask God to speak to you and fill your mouth with wisdom and insight at the appropriate time.

Never forget, however, that a public response to Jesus almost always occurs from within a relationship. In other words, your son probably is not going to wake up one morning and decide to follow Jesus. He must meet Him personally from within the life of another person. Parents need to keep talking about what they're passionate about—in this case, faith in Christ. Ask questions, answer questions, and declare a safe zone to discuss doubts and searchings. All questions are good. All doubts can lead someplace, all searchings provide clues. Our faith can stand up to the inquiry.

Also, do your son a favor—make it your goal at least once during his teen years to state as clearly as possible exactly what you believe and the difference it makes. Don't script or practice it, and don't make it a sales pitch. Just speak from your heart. That's what he's listening to anyway. Fumbled thoughts, lapses, and stammers are gladly welcomed.

Extend an Invitation to a Love Affair

A good friend has spent his entire professional life in leadership development. Not long ago he shared with me the key to sharing Christ with a teenage boy: Make sure our love affair with Jesus is at the point where everyone knows about it and wants to take part too.

My friend used Ephesians 5:15-21 to suggest that we do everything out of our passionate "love affair" with Jesus: "Submit to one another out of reverence for Christ" (v. 21). "Reverence for Christ," he said, "means a love affair. Everyone wants to be part of a love affair, and who better to be in love with?" Amen.

Be extreme in your love, not only to Jesus, but to your young man. Awhile back, Billy Graham had been doing the evening television circuit to promote his autobiography. The host of one particular show was shooting fireball questions at him about faith in Christ and other things. Finally came the hottest question of all: "What do you think of homosexuality?"

Billy Graham thought for a moment and said, "Well, homosexuality is a sin, and it's wrong. But so is pride, envy, lust, covetousness, and others."

"But what would you do if your son told you he was gay?" grilled the anchor.

"I'd love him all the more," Graham replied.

His answer staggered me. I told my kids about that interview the next day, and I also told them that if they announced to me they were gay, I'd love them all the more too.

That shocked them, but I had no idea what it would create until several days later. My son Zac approached me quietly and asked, "Dad, do you sin much?"

His innocent honesty stunned me for a second, and I replied, "Well yes, Zac. I sin all the time."

He was silent for a minute then said, "Yeah, me too. I have something I have to tell you that I've been keeping secret." What unfolded was a simple tale of deception involving a bad situation where he didn't tell me all the details he knew. He felt bad about it and wanted to share that with me.

To be honest, I couldn't have cared less about his misinformation. What I wanted to know was why he chose to tell me. I had a hunch but I wanted to hear it.

To my delight, he said it was the Billy Graham comment. Zac told me that if I would love him more if he was gay, then this little lie should do the same thing. And he was right.

The Father Makes an Offer

My favorite verse of Scripture is at the end of the Bible, in the book of Revelation. In 21:7, John was wrapping up his vision of what will occur in the end times. He quotes God as saying, "He who overcomes will inherit all this, and I will be his God and he will be my son."

I first heard that verse at a very bad time in my life. Those words rescued my flagging spirits, and I believed that promise was for me. I pray that verse will touch you in the same way. Remember today that God is on a mission through time to win your son to Himself. He wants your son, too, to grow both in height and in wisdom. He sees him as an extraordinary young man who is loved by God and all who know him (see Luke 2:52).

As you seek Him daily on behalf of your son, God will make His kingdom the most powerful reality on the planet for your boy.

Chapter Fifteen

Dreamers and Leaders

Your son was made for great things

I write a regular column called "Winners!" for several monthly and weekly newspapers. One that has gotten a lot of response is called, "A Letter to Joe Blow's Parents." Here's some of what I wrote:

Dear Mr. and Mrs. Blow,

I saw your son today and felt compelled to write you this letter. I noticed your boy in the store. He was standing in line waiting to buy several items. I wouldn't have even noticed him had not my eyes accidentally caught his. Something seemed vacant there. I suddenly realized that this young guy was practically invisible to the world. Nothing about him really spoke of life, of energy, or of distinction. He was just another nameless, expressionless face in the crowd. I was overcome by the sense that you, as his folks, should see this moment.

The thing is, there's not a reason in the world for him to blend in like he does. Everything about him is unique and alive and wonderful. I'm certain that unless you tell him, nobody will.

You can teach him to dream bigger, hope larger, see wider, think more. Tell him that people are more afraid of him than he is of them. Ask him to stand erect, chance a look into another's eyes, smile and laugh loudly. It's a mom and dad's job to find the spark in a young man's heart and carefully guard it. You can cradle his hopes and help them come to be...

Don't stand by and let him become some ordinary Joe Blow.

None of us set out to raise a Joe Blow. In fact, if someone were to ask us what we want most for our sons' lives, we'd probably answer that we simply want them to be happy. We want them to fulfill their potential, to see their dreams come true, and to achieve great things for themselves and others.

The good news is that your young man *is* destined for great things. It's your job to help him discover this truth, to raise him to be a dreamer— and a leader.

You need to equip your son to dream and to lead because the two go together. If your son has a dream, he needs leadership skills to make it a goal, then a plan, and then reality. If he's a leader, he needs to have a dream with vision and passion—or nobody will follow.

Dreamers of the Day

I'm not talking about the kind of dreamer who sits around having unrealistic fantasies he never pursues. A true dreamer is a person with vision, passion, and a sense of great purpose. T. E. Lawrence said, "All men dream, but not equally. Those who dream by night in the dusty recesses of their minds awake to find it was vanity. But the dreamers of the day are dangerous men, that they may act their dreams with open eyes to make it possible."

We want to turn ours sons into "dreamers of the day," the opposite of "day dreamers." Let's call them "destiny dreamers." Several things set destiny dreamers apart, including vision, passion, and purpose. Let's look at each of these briefly.

Vision

A destiny dreamer sees visions with shape, color, and dimension. That's what a vision is. It's something you see for yourself in the future. It is the visual aspect of any dream. Maybe your son dreams of being a famous musician. But a vision is more specific. What does he picture? What kind of music does he like? Does he picture himself the object of screaming fans or performing in the London Symphony? Whatever picture it is that your son carries in his head is the vision of his dreams.

Passion

A destiny dream is fueled by emotional energy and desire. If your son says that it would be interesting to be a brain surgeon but he faints at the sight of blood, this probably isn't a destination for him. What does he show great enthusiasm for? What is he willing to invest time and energy in? These are his areas of passion that will fuel his true dreams.

Purpose

A destiny dream involves a deeper motive than money or fame. It is usually wrapped up with your son's desire to change the world for the better. Perhaps his dream of being a basketball star could also involve the desire to make a financial difference in other people's lives, or to be able to get kids' attention so they can be a witness for Christ. If your son can discover the "bigger purpose" to his dreams it, will motivate him to pursue them.

Dream Missiles (seek and develop)

More than anyone else in your son's life, you influence his ability to dream big dreams. Here are a few tools I call "dream missiles" that you can use to influence your son:

Words with Purpose

Teens who have dreams are often embarrassed to share them with someone. In many cases their tendency to hide is right on. Sometimes parents or teachers or siblings feel it's their God-appointed responsibility to "be realistic" and hold a teen's feet on the ground, thus strangling the life out of his aspirations.

Yes, there might come a time when your son needs to hear a bit of your sane mind, but not until you've first shared in the wild, unbridled enthusiasm and possibilities he holds dearly in his heart.

When I speak to groups of teenagers, I warn them about negative parents. I tell them that some parents who were unable to attain many of their dreams subconsciously communicate to their kids that they probably won't be able to attain their dreams either. I encourage teens to ignore this misinformation, and I encourage them to find out for themselves how far they can go and not allow anyone to throw them off the scent.

Encourage the dreamer in your son to stay focused on his big purpose and to keep the picture of the dream he has for himself brightly lit in his mind. These two steps will effectively ward off careless dream killers.

Perhaps your own dream machinery is jammed. Read this list and compare your own self-talk with that of a good dreamer.

Dream Bashers	Dream Blessers
Why?	Why not?
It won't work.	What if it did?
We don't do things that way.	Let's change our ways.
It's impossible.	What if it wasn't?
That's so dumb.	Wow, that's interesting!
You're a dreamer.	You're a genius!
You're just not thinking.	I love it when you dream big.
Give me a break.	Give it to me another way.
That's the stupidest idea.	That's a bright idea.
It'll take you forever.	When can we get started?
It's too far away.	It's closer than you think.
You're just like your dad.	You're just like your mom!
I hope you have a lot of money.	Where can we get a million?
Your mom will never go for this.	I think she just might listen.
Life has ripped me off.	I'll take my life back.

Do yourself a favor and unjam yourself. Change the way you talk about things.

Point Out a Particular Passion or Talent

Most kids fail to dream big because they don't believe in themselves. They can't work up the passion and desire for a big dream when they don't think they're very good at anything.

So what can you do to boost your son's confidence? Encourage him in his areas of interest and achievement. Keep reminding him that there's something special about him. When you say, "Wow, I see you're great at working with your hands," or, "You really love to write, don't you?" you can ignite the passion to fuel a dream.

I once went to a high school track meet where some friends of my kids were competing. One boy wasn't very good, and he took a lot of abuse because of it. He lost a lot of races, but he had a smooth running stride. I thought that with a little coaching he could probably be much better.

I decided to tell him. I approached him and said, "I know a secret about you."

"Which one?" he snapped.

"It's your gait. I don't think you know what a smooth gait you have."

He got interested and asked, "What do you mean?"

"Didn't anyone ever tell you how well you keep your head still as you run?"

"No," he replied. "Our coach doesn't spend any time with me. Is it good to keep my head still?"

"Real good," I said. "It's the sign of a natural runner."

"Nobody ever told me that before."

I believe it. That kid entered every race thereafter with a whole new attitude—and a change in performance too. You see, not very many adults tell young people about their great qualities. They're waiting to be told—desperately, hopefully, prayerfully waiting for someone to find something good about them and tell them. They're brewing now, waiting for someone to tell them what they'll become. Will it be you?

Show Him a Vision

Introduce your son to some optimistic dreamers. A very good friend of mine is a missionary building contractor named Homer Lininger. Homer is one of our generation's true saints. He's built churches and schools for missionaries around the world, eaten with headhunters, had machine guns shoved in his face by revolutionaries, and eaten bugs to survive. All for his love of Christ.

Having dinner with Homer is no ordinary meal. Discussions swing wildly from the flavor of hippopotamus meat to ducking poison-tipped blow darts. Here is a man who can tell stories as big as life. This is stuff even teenagers love.

We need to introduce our sons to men like this, men who can demonstrate dreams as big as life. That's where visions get clarified and detailed.

Recruit interesting people and invite them to your house. Dreamers love to share their dreams. People who live want others to live too. Meet them where you can, find them on the Internet, read books and magazines about them.

Spend some time expanding your own vision. When was the last time you were ablaze with vision and excitement? If it hasn't been in the last several hours, then you need a recharge.

From Dreamer to Leader

Dreams and visions fuel our kids to achieve their destiny. But many kids who dream end up slamming into real life—and quitting. Their visions of being a great basketball star crash when they don't make the starting lineup their senior year. Gradually they give up dreaming.

Why? Because their destiny dreams never materialized into goals, then into plans, and then into reality. They failed the greatest leadership test of their lives: the ability to lead the way in fulfilling their own destinies.

There are many kinds of leadership, but I'm not talking about running meetings, organizing committees, or leading a group of guys into a war zone. I'm talking about the kind of leadership essential to every young man who wants his dream to become his destiny.

The kind of leaders I'm referring to know how:

- To turn a desired end into a goal. A goal is really just a dream in the hands of a leader.

- To come up with a plan. Having a goal is not enough. A leader wants to see his goal realized, so he plans a set of steps and a course of action to help him get there.
- To enlist the help of others. No one can achieve his dreams alone. A leader in charge of his destiny will enlist the help and support of many—teachers, institutions, and fellow-dreamers.

Helping Your Teen Become This Kind of Leader

The obstacles your son faces in becoming a leader are similar to those he faces when it comes to dreaming big—only worse. In pursuing his dreams, your son risks only embarrassment. In leading, he risks public failure!

But leadership is a practical skill that you can help your son learn in a variety of ways.

Give Pivotal Support (at key moments)

For most of their lives, teenage boys try to fit in and find their places among their peers, and they fear intentionally breaking ranks. But as with most things, the fear of loneliness is much worse than the truth of it. The difference between a young man who steps forward and tries and one who doesn't is often an adult who offers some pivotal encouragement.

Once my son Jake was on the verge of doing something that for him was very daring and very lonely. Before he left home, I gave him a three-by-five card with one of my favorite quotes on it:

"Be bold, and mighty forces will come to your aid."

He later shared with me that the quote gave him courage at a moment when he was very afraid.

Provide Home-Front Opportunities

Remember, a leader turns a dream or desire into a goal. Give your son opportunities to formulate a goal and then figure out steps to get there.

Your son's number-one resource is you. The space between you is a place to talk, learn, share, and scheme. A place your son wants to come to rather than flee from. A place of power. A place of refueling. A place of confidence.

You can help nurture this by speaking of and referring to leadership often. Pepper the air with words like *leadership, vision, strength,* and *faith.* Make these terms part of your everyday vocabulary. Great actions are often preceded by a vocabulary change.

If you give your son the opportunity to be in front, to lead the pack, to think himself the captain of his ship from time to time, he'll be a better man for it. Tell him:

- "John, you're in charge of figuring out how to change the oil in the car."
- "Ben, I want you to lead our family in a discussion about vacations and help us come up with a plan for compromise."

To help him progress, alternate your patience and prods. Be kind and draw it out.

Expect Success

Remember, a leader has a goal, which is a dream with the attached expectation of achieving it. To help develop uncommon leadership in your son, personally expect it. But be sure to make it a positive expectation. Have you ever heard yourself say, "Don't be bad… Don't be a loser… Don't do…"? Those sorts of expectations don't create strength and certainty. Those are negative "run from" expectations. Try to create positive "go to" expectations. "What are you going to say if they ask you to lead a discussion?" or, "There's a good chance you'll be the one to help organize this."

Young men perform better with positive expectations. Some of these expectations you will never even mention. You transmit them in the way you act. Your son reads the signals clearly. Just ask him.

Questions are another good way to communicate expectations. Good questions might be, "What would you do in this matter?" or "What do you think I should do?" These questions catch teens off guard because

---

A Closer Focus

Payback Time

In our home, money is loaned often in all directions. If my son has borrowed money from me and fails to pay it back when he's promised it three times, I tack on 50 percent interest. I don't collect with a baseball bat (and I'm not talking about borrowing a buck for a Coke). I just casually mention the interest penalty for procrastination and leave it there. It works well after the first few times.

Look on debt as work in the bank. Our kids work off their debts by typing, order fulfillment, phone calls, cleaning, and running errands. I strike a deal, normally strongly in my favor, and they work it off. In almost every case, my boys would prefer to work off their debts rather than part with their cash.

Bad debts can be worked off on behalf of someone other than you. For instance, your son borrows fifteen dollars to buy a CD and doesn't pay you back. Rather than force him to pay, you might ask him to pull fifteen dollars' worth of weeds for a friend. Or help his mother.

they're used to being told what to do, not consulted. Young leaders need to be groomed by asking them for their thoughtful input.

Another question I ask is, "What does your decision say about you?" When I first began asking this question of my teenagers, they stonewalled me. They'd shoot me that trademark adolescent shrug accompanied by an, "I dunno." But I'm ruthless. I kept it up, subtly and relentlessly. I simply wanted to provoke their thinking.

Recently I discovered how well this question functions when I heard my elder son cross-examining his brother about a dumb decision he'd made. In the midst of their interchange, guess what I heard? You bet.

Give Him a Little Push

Some of the greatest experiences I had growing up were when some loving adult shoved me into the path of an onrushing education. Jesus "shoved" people that way. Early in His ministry He had His greenhorn disciples preaching, healing the sick, managing travel arrangements, controlling crowds, and a host of other things they'd never done! Jesus wasn't too hot on sitting around planning. He believed in faith-based action. He always watched what God was doing and then, with little thought to details, hustled after it.

Is it possible you're being too careful with your teenager? Are there opportunities to push him into the path of experience, like you might push a reluctant kid into a pool? It doesn't have to be harsh. Let me tell you a story to show you how it works.

Several years ago I wanted to show my son Zac how to shoot a .22 rifle. He was pretty nervous but excited about his opportunity to graduate from water pistols. Typically, I'm methodical about teaching these things, but this time I figured I'd conduct a leadership seminar with him.

Prior to this, Zac had never handled the rifle. It was a family rule. When we arrived at the range, without warning I pulled the gun out of its case and handed it to Zac. Then I asked him to use all he knew about guns to check whether it was loaded, then load the clip, insert the clip, and fire several rounds. I told him I was there only for emergency guidance and to be sure he didn't hurt himself or others. And finally, I said, "Zac, I know you're nervous, and you should be. You can hear about guns all day long, but you have to have an experience with a gun to learn. You can do this. Go slow and ask questions."

He did great, and I'm sure he learned his lessons at a profoundly deep level.

Sometimes leadership needs to be learned by experience. Leadership cannot be explained in academic exercises. It must be felt and touched. Like public speaking, the more you experience it, the better you get.

Look for Unseen Pockets of Power

Remember, a leader knows how to enlist others to help him achieve goals. Often your son will respond to other people more powerfully than to you. Don't be offended or hurt. It's normal. Begin searching for what I call "pockets of power." Right now, all around you are groups of parents and young leaders doing great things with teenagers. They're in local churches, YMCAs, 4-H clubs, Young Life, Youth for Christ, Boy Scouts, Athletes in Action, Youth Conservation League, Junior Achievement, and many more organizations.

Inside these groups are young men and women your son will connect with. These people are organized for and committed to building your son into a leader. All you need to do is arrange transportation, give thanks to God for people like this, and get out of the way. It's a good deal. Go find some of them.

Passing Through to Greatness

This book has been an epic journey for me. I hate to see it end. The good news is that it's not ending. I mentioned early in this book that teenagers have been like they are forever. There will never be a shortage of teenagers passing through this short but vital time in life. The only shortage is parents willing to be strong, decisive, creative, and faithful to the end.

I pray that you are one of those parents. You are going to live the major portion of your life with an adult child, not a teenage child. I pray that this book helps prepare the way for a life together that you can both be happy and satisfied about. I think that's going to happen. God bless you and your awesome boy!

PART FIVE

_____

SHAPING A MAN'S FUTURE

Chapter Sixteen

Answers to Typical Parent Issues

The main thing is you're not alone

I lead a lot of seminars on raising teen boys, and I field lots of e-mail from parents like you. In the process I'm always surprised by the similarity of the problems we face regardless of geography, family size, or personal history. People raising teenagers in Maine are struggling with the same issues that face parents in California. Older parents are just as confused as younger ones. Solo parents and intact couples have identical concerns. We're all fighting the same battles, which means that none of us is alone.

That's why I wanted to collect the most frequently asked questions about raising teenage boys. The following three chapters in this updated edition contain my best answers to the questions most parents of teenage boys are asking.

But first, before we start talking about your teenage son, let's talk about you. Every parent carries some heavy—and unwanted—baggage. And you can be sure your teenager will use it against you if he can! Too many parents shrink from the responsibility of effectively parenting their teenage boys because they're embarrassed by their own past mistakes. We're all guilty of being fallen creatures; we've all done things we now regret. So let's take care of some personal housekeeping.

Skeletons in Your Closet

I once received the saddest e-mail from a dad who was struggling with kleptomania (the uncontrollable urge to steal things). He couldn't leave a store without carrying something out that he hadn't paid for. He'd been caught shoplifting as a young person, but he continued committing petty theft as an adult. He was remorseful about not shaking this compulsion, and he asked me how he could hold his son to a higher standard when he himself was guilty of repeated sin.

My suggestion to him applies to every parent, whether your problem is cheating on your taxes, habitual lying, or carrying on a secret life of lust, gambling, or addiction. The first step is to put an end to your wrong behavior. Stop stealing, lying, gambling, sleeping around, or whatever your particular struggle is. If you've tried repeatedly and failed, then get professional help. Stop wringing your hands and fretting. Start fixing things for good. There's no reason you can't do that right now. And while you're gaining victory, stop using your sullied past as an excuse for a continued lack of resolve today.

The truth is we all have a past that we're not entirely proud of. Find me a person who says he has nothing to hide, and I'll show you a liar. Sure, some people have more skeletons in the closet than others, but pretending that you've never messed up will rob you of power. Pretending to be something you're not will steal your confidence as a parent. Consistency of character and a straight line between your beliefs and actions are the stuff of integrity. And personal integrity breeds confidence.

To regain the confidence you need to be an effective parent, start by being honest. Admit that you are, in fact, a hypocrite. We all are. A quick review of your life will reveal instances of breaking many, if not most, of the Ten Commandments. This is part of your history and can't be changed. But it *can* be forgiven—by God and by those you have wronged. Forgiveness restores your confidence as a parent, so let me offer some guidelines on putting your history behind you.

Begin by admitting that you're guilty. If you have wronged friends or family members, confess to them and seek their forgiveness. Say to those you have wronged: I'm guilty; I have wronged you; please forgive me. And pray to God, humbly admitting your sinfulness and seeking His forgiveness. I can tell you from personal experience that something happens within you when you have the humility and guts to "stand down" and just admit what you did. Your teenage son needs a parent who will raise him in confidence and integrity. So drop the weight of the things that hold you down by asking forgiveness, and parent your son with your head held high.

I know firsthand how hard it is to put your past behind you. I feel so guilty about some things that I tend to resort to self-inflicted torture. But understandable or not, hanging our heads in shame does a disservice to our sons. I've found that being perfectly honest and up-front with mature, thinking teenagers opens a vast range of new possibilities for deeper relationships. Now is not the time to hide things or to hide behind the excuse of our own checkered past.

Our sons know we're not perfect, so it's natural for them to ask some hard questions. They want to know if we've ever blown it, and trying to duck the question won't help the situation. So take a deep breath and be transparent with your son. Without giving all the lurid details, share what has happened in your own life.

This type of vulnerability does two things. First, it lets your teenage boy know that you're a flawed human just like he is. Your son may be shocked by your admission of past failures. But more often a teenager will be comforted in knowing that if a parent is forthright about his or her own flaws, it frees him to be up-front about his own personal struggles. He no longer needs to hide things from you. The clear message that is sent by a parent's openness is a crucial one: Life's failures and embarrassments can be handled, and grace and forgiveness can be extended to anyone regardless of how bad they've been.

When you admit your own failings, your son can no longer accuse you of being merely the petty judge of his life, the jury rigged to convict him, and the jailer out to extract retribution for his crimes. You are now a fellow struggler who is seeking to live with integrity. So take the risk of being honest with your son. You and he both will reap the rewards of a genuine relationship, one that is free of secrecy and hypocrisy.

Solo Parenting a Teenage Man

Raising a teenage son as a team of two is a daunting task even for the best of parents. But raising one alone can quickly become overwhelming. Single parents are short on time, low on energy, and quickly running out of money. Add to that an "empty" reading on the tank of emotional reserves, and you've got a recipe for extreme burnout.

If you're a single parent, you might have just enough energy to twitch in agreement—or maybe even to grunt an "amen" to that! Single parents need hope, confidence, and a plan of action. So my advice is simple and centered around one core theme: Life is a long road with many opportunities to win back what you've lost. Focus on winning what you can and forgive yourself for the rest.

The loneliness and confusion you feel are compounded by exhaustion and guilt (when you have the time to stop and think about it). And that's just you! Your son is also experiencing a range of emotions: hopelessness, aimlessness, sadness, and confusion. He might feel that he is responsible for one parent being absent from the family. If so, he is bearing a tremendous load of undeserved guilt.

Or he may be delirious with excitement that he's a teenager with the world before him and an overworked parent who is too busy to look over his shoulder all the time. The combination of heavy cares and exhilarating freedom is a confusing combination for a teenage boy to handle. Meanwhile, you want to be the parent your son needs while also keeping yourself together. All of this requires the wisdom of Solomon.

Feeling overwhelmed is normal. You're not superhuman; you're one person tackling one of life's biggest challenges all by yourself. Since you're making decisions alone and stretching yourself thin to cover all the bases, conserve your energy and maintain your sanity. You can't win every battle, so settle for winning those you can. And remember that most battles aren't even worth fighting. So conserve your energy for the crucial engagements. And while you're picking your battles, don't allow heartache and negative situations to sap your strength.

Allow me to make some specific suggestions to get this done. First, stay in shape physically. Set aside ten minutes a day for aerobic activity. Don't tell me you haven't got the time! Aerobic action gives you more energy than sleeping. Being in minimally good aerobic health helps you blow off steam and makes you a better parent. Watch your fat and sugar intake too. Slim, healthy people tell me this is the key to more energy.

Second, establish and attain one goal a day (a parental goal would be great). Make it simple, like spending twenty quality minutes with your kids. Then, if you set the goal, move heaven and earth to accomplish it. Beleaguered single parents are always surprised by the rush they get when they achieve something they've set their minds to do. And success breeds success. Single parents don't get many opportunities to shine, so sometimes you have to create your own. Set an attainable goal today and achieve it. Then do it again tomorrow. You'll be amazed at what a boost you'll get.

Third, remember that time is one of life's great pharmaceuticals. Time may be the only salve that will heal the tremendous number of wounds you sustain in the wrenching experience of divorce and raising kids alone. Develop a long-range outlook on when things will begin to improve. Things *will* get better; they always do. The time will come when you'll laugh again, when things will seem normal again, when you'll have a life again. Keep your eyes up and let God show you the hopes that lie out on the horizon.

Moms Raising Teenage Men

As a former clinical psychotherapist, I'm often asked about the psychological impact on boys when they are raised by single women. This question usually relates to the mother-son dynamic, giving rise to images from Oedipus, Freud, and sundry other imagined dangers. Will a boy become warped somehow as a result of not having a father figure around on a regular basis? Will a strong mother figure make it more likely that a boy will exhibit homosexual tendencies? In the absence of a resident father, will a boy develop an unnatural emotional attachment to his mother? And that's just the A-list of worries!

Complex theories about all of this have been expounded by smart-looking guys in tweed jackets, with chins begging to be stroked. High-minded *sounding* theories can create unnecessary fear and uncertainty in women who have no choice but to raise their young men alone. So remember what theories are: just untested, wild-eyed guesses. I've got good news for you: It's not as difficult as you've been led to believe. A loving and committed single parent is far superior to two resident parents who are so caught up in their own lives that they neglect their children's needs.

Still, there is an element of challenge here. All young men need a man in their lives. There are things boys need that only a man can impart. For example, men tend to be much harder on boys than mothers are. Men are physically more intimidating and somehow are able to get your son to do things that you've tried your best at but failed. The man might use the exact same words you would, but for some reason your son responds to him and blows you off. I can't explain it (though I have some pretty snazzy theories!). I just know it happens.

If you have a brother or a close male friend, see if he would be willing to mentor your son. You might have to be forthright and ask many times. Just do it! Men and boys can connect through common interests: basketball, cars, hiking, skiing, hunting, or fishing. Your son will enjoy spending time with a man, and it'll give you a break. It also shows your son that other adults are interested in him and want him to succeed.

As a single mom, there's no escaping the fact that you will be the most influential adult in your son's life. Don't panic! I know many men who were raised exclusively by mothers and turned out great. How did that happen? Their moms supplied some simple things these young men needed the most in their teenage years.

First, encourage your son to seek out men who are a natural part of his life. With a bit of encouragement, your son will put himself in positions where he can have a relationship with an uncle, grandfather, coach, teacher, or youth group worker. Though most boys are shy about asking a man to befriend them, a little encouragement from you goes a long way. Often a boy feels an allegiance to his mother and thinks that getting close to a man who isn't his father would be the same as abandoning her. Make sure he knows that is not the case. Cheer him on and mean it!

Second, begin the process of letting him go. Teenage boys are well past the time when they need you for physical survival. If you believe your son needs you desperately, those are probably your own insecurities talking. While he may rely on you for clean laundry, well-balanced meals, and transportation (if he's younger than sixteen), he's much more independent and self-reliant than you realize. He doesn't need you to do everything, so give yourself a break.

Third, remember that at this age, your son's peer group is probably more important to him than any father figure might be. Teenage boys, regardless of their home situation, rely on their friends for advice, input, and identity. In light of this, it makes more sense for you to worry about your son's peers than the fact that no man is around.

Fourth, remember that there are many scenarios far worse than your raising your son alone. It's better to have no man around than to have your son emulate an irresponsible, abusive man who would teach him false lessons about life.

It wasn't a mistake that God made you the mother of your son, so take a measure of confidence from this. Assume your full authority and don't be a pushover. You have a much stronger hand than you may be used to using, and you're fully equipped and qualified to use all your talents to be a strong, resourceful, capable mom. That's what young men need! Stand up and do your best no matter how incapable you feel. Nobody feels fully capable, so you're not alone. Be tough when necessary, be loving when you sense the need, and trust your gut. You can do this!

The Stepparent Challenge

Let's get this out of the way right up-front: Stepparenting and blending families is tough, demanding, hard work. You've got a world of forces working against you, no matter how happy you and your new spouse are together. Kids, no matter how unhappy the original marriage was, want their biological parents to be reunited. Obviously, your marriage to someone else makes that impossible, and this gives rise to all sorts of unpredictable behavior in kids. Even if you're a saint, it won't be easy to avoid being tagged as the devil.

Your greatest ally is time. Most people who have lived through the tumultuous first five years of a remarriage tell me that things do smooth out, but not until they've endured a parade of traumas. Therefore, your greatest challenges are patience and keeping a long-range perspective. After suffering a few years of bumps, pettiness, and unfairness of all types, your family environment will finally settle into a normal rhythm.

When it comes to connecting with stepsons, you need to draw on three resources: time, availability, and patience. You can't force teenagers to like you. It's nothing personal; they just disapprove of you because of what you represent. It's like handling an injured animal. You can't just scoop it up in your arms. If you try, the animal will bite you. Rather, you have to go slow, talk and console, endure the occasional snaps and nips, and in time the injured creature will warm up. The winner in the stepparenting game is the person with the most patience. Make sure that person is you.

The Problem of Peers' Parents

Ironically, one of the toughest parenting challenges has nothing at all to do with your kids. It involves the parents of your kids' friends. Some parents just aren't to be trusted, and chances are your son likes those parents the most!

As the father of two teenage sons, I have no tolerance for blatant stupidity in full-grown adults. I've seen parents do brazenly idiotic things in an effort to appear hip and with it. Why? The only reason I can find is that they're afraid of driving their sons away by being strong, decisive, and clear.

What these parents fail to realize is that all people—teenagers included—respond favorably to intelligent leadership and direction that helps everybody win. Teens don't seek out adults who are just like them; instead they tend to seek out accessible, relaxed, "fun" adults who they can communicate with and feel comfortable around. These are not the parents who let their teens throw wild parties, bring their girlfriends over to spend the night, and pass around a joint at family gatherings. In fact, these kinds of parents aren't respected at all…just used for the freedom they permit.

The good news is that most parents are smart enough to be adults around their teens. The bad news is that there are a few parents who have been knocked wacky with the idiot stick. You have no doubt encountered them. If some of your son's friends have these folks for parents, keep the following in mind.

First, don't let yourself get so torqued up at the lunacy you see around you that you can't function. Rather, set your own standards and clearly spell them out for your son. Remember the adage I use often in this book: "You can't control everything, so control what you can."

Second, clear expectations for behavior are essential. Your son needs to know the rules and standards ahead of time. And he needs to know the penalties for violating family rules. Clear expectations will help minimize confusion over what's acceptable and what is not. It's helpful to write down the expectations and post them in a well-traveled area. The front of the refrigerator is a good spot.

Finally, once the rules are in place, be ready to deal with violations of the established standards. Don't be wishy-washy when your son tests your resolve, but use wisdom in responding to unacceptable behavior.

Be unbending on certain rules, especially involving immoral behavior, breaking the law, and any behavior that threatens your son's health and safety or the well-being of those around him. In other matters, be open to discussion. Give your son a chance to explain why he failed to abide by a certain rule. He might actually have a valid reason. Perhaps it's time to amend the rule due to changing circumstances. An open conversation about the rightness of your rules makes you much easier for him to deal with.

Make certain that your son knows in advance which standards are set in stone and which are open to dialogue. Again, I suggest you do this in writing. Your son should know that you're aware of the big picture and thinking fairly about the standards you enforce.

Since family rules apply to your son even when he's away from home, make it plain which of his friends' parents have standards that vary from yours. Your son may assume that if another parent allows a certain behavior, it's acceptable. He must know that although you are trying as hard as you can to accommodate him, some things just don't cut it. If he violates a nonnegotiable family rule when he's away from home, he'll have to pay the price.

When Grandparents Raise Teenagers

Few things tug at my heart more than a grandmother herding two or three wild grandchildren through a store. Her weary shuffle and frazzled looks tell the story. Grandparents are supposed to be able to give the kids back when they get tired of them, but you can't give the kids back if they're living at your house!

I don't need to tell you that keeping up with young people can be exhausting. So acknowledge the age difference and don't try to keep up with them. Just do the best you can. Teenagers will recognize your effort, and if they don't, ask that they cooperate with you because you're tired. Most normal teenage boys will respond to such a direct request. If not, see chapter 8, "911—Help!" which deals with troubled teens.

Once you acknowledge your age and the inherent limitations related to it, remember the power that you exert. The greatest force in the physical universe is low-level, relentless pressure. You may very well be the most stable, persistent force in your grandson's life. If you have him in your custody, chances are good that he has been through some major life trauma. If you establish yourself as a source of reliability, you'll have great power to shape his life forever. Healthy teenagers find fair, happy, open-minded older people to be irresistible. Here's an incredible opportunity that you shouldn't take lightly. Don't expect your teenage grandson to thank you constantly for your sacrifices on his behalf—he's not even aware of them yet. But he will be. Be patient, and it will come.

Also, take heart in the fact that teenagers help keep you young! Kids have a boundless supply of vitality, open-mindedness, and excitement about the future. These are things that adults need more of. With the proper attitude, you may come to see raising a teenage grandson as one of the most vital and exciting times of your life.

Chapter Seventeen

Answers to Typical Problems with Teenage Boys

Self-esteem, entertainment choices, lying, discipline, and other issues

Teenage boys are a wild blend of electronics, tattoos, stylish little jewelry in oddly placed holes, weird hair, baggy pants, Doc Martens, hip-hop, and heaven knows what else. But while styles and tastes change dramatically with each generation, most of the challenges you face in parenting your teenage son are no different from the obstacles faced by any parent of any teenager in the last fifty years. Teenage men have always needed to establish an identity that is separate and distinct from their parents. They still tend to approach life as if their personal concerns are the most important issues of all time. And teens like to experiment and take risks that baffle and frighten their parents. Sometimes they even do it on purpose! These things are normal and haven't changed for generations.

One teenage boy might present more of a challenge than another, but the range of parenting issues that crop up most regularly is remarkably uniform among all teenage boys. So relax, take a deep breath, and walk with me through these frequently asked questions about raising perfectly normal teenagers.

Music, Movies, and the Internet

Several elements of our culture have changed drastically since you and I came up through the teenage ranks. The biggest changes have to do with technology, access to information, and the loss of parental control over what is available to teenagers. In the "old days," as long ago as the early 1990s, parents had near total control over what types of "entertainment" crept into their homes. We could lock out certain stations on cable television or decide not to subscribe to cable at all. We could monitor what types of CDs our kids were buying. We could be reasonably sure that if our son wanted to rent a sexually oriented video or buy a pornographic magazine, he'd have to come up with some very slick scheme to get it.

But not today. If your home computer is connected to the Internet, your teenager has ready access to the full range of music, literature, and visual images—offensive and otherwise. Pornography, violence, and explicit language are just a mouse click away. Our homes are no longer a safe haven from unwholesome influences. We're inundated with raunch, and it won't change. So we'd better deal with it.

It has been noted that the youth culture is preoccupied with entertainment. How true. For many teens, entertainment invests life with meaning. Too many kids are simply unable to cope in a world that's not constantly keeping them entertained. And television, music, computer games, and DVDs are just the beginning. The Internet and its computer-based sideshows will only multiply in the years to come.

While we're still in the infancy of this technology, we need to decide to control it before it controls us. And I don't mean that in a negative way. I'm excited about how computers will change our lives for the good. Some of the miracles we'll see are medical care administered over the Internet, personal safety and security vastly improved, working environments that are more advantageous to family life, and much more. Now is the time to take your place at the head of the Internet/entertainment parade.

First, remember that we'll eventually get into a rhythm with this new entertainment culture (Internet/movies/music). That happens when the newness and the initial shock of it all wears off, and we find that it wasn't such a big deal in the first place. But rather than just fall into a rhythm set by someone else, go ahead and establish the rhythm yourself. How? Set time limits on all your household electronics—video games, TV, computer, CD player, DVD player. You'd set limits on anything your son did if he appeared to be obsessed with it. If he is filling too much of his time (and his mind) with entertainment to the detriment of school- work, creative pursuits, helping others, and deepening relationships, then it's reasonable to set a time limit.

Second, be more concerned about what's in your son's heart than where his mouse is pointing. Is your son's Net surfing mere idle curiosity or an unhealthy habit? The way to find out is to delve into the entertainment culture with your son.

The reason that sex, violence, and bad music are such a threat to us as parents is that we're afraid these influences will bend our kids in the wrong direction. Though our kids are susceptible to incremental steps toward depravity, they're probably more firmly grounded in what's right and wrong than you might think. They toy with "badness" out of curiosity, but most teen boys won't plunge into a lifestyle of debauchery just from watching R-rated movies or singing rap lyrics.

De-emphasize the "badness" of things, preferring instead to discuss what all this means for your son's life in the bigger picture. He won't enjoy these conversations with you at first, but you can be sure he'll be thinking about them later. The important thing is that your son knows it's all right to talk with you about it.

A third step is to challenge your son to contribute something of his own to the entertainment culture. Encourage him to write his own songs and play his music for others, rather than just passively listening to music the record companies want to sell him. If he's spending too much time watching movies, suggest that he write a script, assemble a cast, and grab a camcorder to create his own cinematic work of art. If he's drawn to the Internet, what sites is he visiting? Have him utilize his computer skills to create his own Web site (nonsexual of course).

Combat the negative influence of the entertainment culture by tapping into your son's creative abilities, areas of interest, and passion. Your encouragement and assistance, when needed, will go a long way in keeping your son from being a passive consumer of whatever the entertainment world wants to feed him.

Harmful Entertainment

After reading the previous answer, some of you may be convinced that I've got my head in the sand. You may be fighting a much more serious war over explicit sex, extreme violence, and demeaning music. For your son, a few suggestions about moderation and using his creative abilities to fashion his own entertainment will be a waste of breath.

If your son is immersed in sex, violence, and dehumanizing music, you have to draw a clear and absolute line. No offensive material will be allowed in your home, period. When you specify what will henceforth be forbidden, always speak from the "I" perspective. Avoid condemning and accusatory messages using the word *you*. For instance, say to your son: "I'm not comfortable with your watching R-rated videos, visiting a 'hot sex' Web site, and listening to music that advocates rape and other forms of violence. Since these things contradict the values of our family, I won't allow them in our house."

Don't beat him up for his choice of entertainment. Instead, make these discussions about rules positive and productive. Keep the focus on what you, as the adult in charge, want and don't want in your home. It's not necessary to lay a guilt trip on your son in order to set a standard in your home. Will he like it? No, he'll most likely kick and fuss. But keep talking about how the things we're exposed to influence our thinking and our attitudes, and insist that you won't allow yourself or members of your family to be influenced by messages of violence, degradation, and demeaning sex.

If you own the TV, DVD player, computer, and telephone, you have every right, actually an *obligation,* to control how these things are used. If your son owns the equipment, you have the right to control the electricity that runs it, the house that houses it…you get the idea.

When Teens Blame Parents

Teenagers (and kids in general) are experts at making *their* problems look as though they're *yours.* They don't make a conscious decision to pass the buck; it's a more gradual process. To turn this habit around, you need to recognize the process and then find ways to guide conversations in a new direction.

If you look at the situation realistically, you can respond with understanding rather than retaliation and bitterness. When your teenager assigns blame in your direction, he isn't actually doing anything to you. He is only doing what you're allowing him to do. You're actually agreeing to be a victim.

Here's a common exchange between teenager and parent. You ask him to clean up his room, and he retaliates by saying he hasn't got time because you've asked him to do so many other chores. You get defensive and begin explaining why you've asked him to do the other chores, and he responds with additional excuses. You feel compelled to offer more and more defenses to justify all the things you've asked him to do. By the time this process has cycled two or three times, you're back on your heels trying to explain virtually everything you've done in the past several weeks. You get madder and madder, which makes you look even more wrong.

Now that you're backed into a corner, you have two choices. You can force your son to do the thing he insists is unjust and completely your fault, or you can let him off the hook and do it yourself. Neither outcome is what you're looking for. But parents are driven to this point because we allow ourselves to be put on the defensive right from the start.

This is fairly easy to solve. Keep your mind clear and don't allow yourself to get defensive. Learn to listen to what your son is saying, then think before you respond. There is no need for you to defend your reasons for asking your son to help out around the house. You provide food, clothing, the comfort and security of a home. A teenager shares the responsibility of doing his part to help the household run smoothly. He owes you.

So the justification for asking a teenager to do chores, run errands, keep his room in order, help out with younger siblings, or take care of yard work is simply "because I asked." Don't get suckered into a war of words to justify why you've asked Johnny to lift a finger. Teach your son that he is expected to do things around the house because you've asked. Period. If he complains that you're a monster and it's all your fault, agree with him that you are in fact the one who requires him to do all this work. Then tell him to go straighten his room. End of conversation. This approach puts an end to needless arguments, which only get you entangled in a no-win bind.

Coping with Sibling Rivalry

Fighting with siblings, competing for attention, blaming brothers and sisters for the teen's own missteps. If you have more than one child, you know the routine. The good news is that sibling rivalry typically is more pronounced with younger teenagers. Many of the mechanics that keep sibling rivalry alive die out with the onset of higher-level cognitive thinking (which first appears at the outset of adolescence). After the teen years begin in earnest, siblings usually find that aligning themselves with a brother is far superior to competing with him. In other words, having an ally during conflicts with parents is preferable to picking a fight with your sibling. Solomon said, "A brother is born for adversity" (Proverbs 17:17), and boys begin to understand this intuitively in the teen years.

If your kids are older teens and you still face the problem of sibling rivalry, here are some things to consider. Most teenagers begin the process of defining who they are by rebelling against the people in their world. This process of differentiation is most pronounced with those closest to them—their parents and other family members. A teen needs to push away from you in order to get a better look at himself. That pushing-away process occurs between siblings, too, especially if one of the teens is deemed superior in some way—a better athlete, a more gifted student, a more popular kid at school.

Your response to this should be the same no matter what the situation: You need to help each of the battling sibs discover his own independent identity. Spend some time with each child finding out about his own unique take on the world, his hopes, dreams, wishes. In doing this you begin the long process of helping your son discover who he is in his own right, standing alone, being known for his own talents and abilities and strengths. Identity can be established by looking inward, recognizing the person God created him to be, not by fighting a brother to establish superiority or to demand respect.

Also remember that competition and greed lead to sibling fights. Most people believe that the things of value in life are limited, so they feel they must scratch and claw to obtain as much as they can. In contrast, people who believe that things of value are available in abundance don't feel the need to fight. They know that the important things (including respect, love, attention, affection) are in plentiful supply. If they need more, they can just go get some more! Your role in helping your sons adopt the latter view is to make sure you are dispensing plenty of attention, love, time, and involvement in both their lives. If their emotional tanks have been filled with parental love and involvement, they are less likely to believe that they have to fight to claim a shrinking slice of a very small pie.

Finally, you don't need me to tell you that boys by nature are combative and competitive. They're going to mix it up from time to time, so teach them that they need to fight with respect. The conflict revolves around issues, not personalities. If they reach an impasse and feel they absolutely must fight it out (which happens occasionally), they have to take it outside. These incidents will be rare, since boys don't like pain and they'd rather be friends. But when all else fails to bring them together, get out of the way and let them settle it for themselves.

Punishing Teenage Boys

Discipline for teenagers is really more about shaping good behavior than about punishment of misdeeds. Your teenage man will soon be living on his own, making decisions alone, taking responsibility for his life in a cold, unforgiving world. Your job in the teen years is to do what you can to prepare him for success as an adult. That involves disciplining him from time to time. Unfortunately, most parents are very uncomfortable and unfamiliar with techniques that work to discipline the young men in their family.

If you've read the previous chapters of this book, you know that I'm a fan of "disengagement." In its simplest form, disengagement involves making your position clear, restating your expectations for your son's behavior, and then refusing to be drawn into a useless debate. If your son persists in trying to argue the point, you simply walk away. (See chapter 6 for a full description of how this works.) I will admit, though, that I'm hearing from a lot of parents who are reluctant to use this technique, mostly because it seems so *mean*.

Let me address this perception. As you read this book right now, your emotional level is probably fairly steady. You're not feeling threatened, angry, or fearful. Hopefully, you are feeling growing confidence and optimism. Because you're not embroiled right now in a heated exchange with your son, the thought of applying disengagement might seem mean or even borderline abusive.

Now try to put yourself in the emotional cauldron that boils whenever you and your son lock horns over family rules, your need for help around the house, or his failure to keep you informed of his whereabouts. When you're faced with an uncooperative, irascible teen, your state of mind changes. At that moment the prospect of making yourself clear and then refusing to engage in further debate will show itself to be more fair-minded and less "abusive" than raising your voice, pointing your finger, and saying things in anger that you'll regret later. Our judgments of what's appropriate change depending on the circumstances. So let me suggest that you at least give disengagement a try whenever you feel that further discussion is likely to lead to an unproductive shouting match. Your son wants to have the last word, and so do you. Don't give in to this urge. Just make yourself clear and then walk away. When you refuse to be drawn into a needless argument, you're letting your actions speak for themselves.

Let me suggest one more thing: Disengagement isn't mean, it's tough. Remember, the idea is to let your kid know how lucky he is to have you around (and that his luck could easily run out). Your son will soon be on his own, and disengagement is the safest, most intelligent way I know of teaching teenagers about the real world.

The Self-Esteem Problem

I'm bothered by all the hoopla over self-esteem. Ask ten people to define it, and you'll get eleven different answers, resulting in lots of confusion. Most people will say that self-esteem is how you feel about yourself. Others say it's self-perception. Both of these are what I consider to be "soft," impossible-to-measure internal states that people experience.

Then there is the argument that self-esteem breeds better behavior and higher performance. Has anyone conclusively linked feeling good about yourself to the ability to improve the world around you? Not by a long shot! Adolf Hitler felt great about himself and had an amazing impact on his world. Tragically, six million Jews died as a result. All the research I've read leaves me very suspicious of the whole concept of self-esteem.

Another reason I don't like the idea of self-esteem is that it, like so many other psychological concepts, was made up out of thin air. Many experts in the field of linguistics believe that when you name something, it comes into being. When you describe it, it comes to life. Self-esteem as an independent force exists only in our minds and in our words. We've made ourselves slaves to something that isn't real.

So why all the talk about it? Most parents want their teenagers to like themselves, to esteem themselves highly. That's fine. We should encourage kids to like themselves, but it makes no sense to do this in a vacuum. To be sure, God loves us. The Bible is clear that this alone makes us valuable. God created us as people of tremendous worth. But God saved us so that we might expend ourselves in the service of others. This is not esteeming yourself, but esteeming others. Self-esteem doesn't exist alone; it comes as a result of producing something that benefits someone else.

Teenagers are in an excellent position to produce value in the lives of others. They can extend friendship, exhibit kindness, pitch in and help when assistance is needed, side with the underdog who has no one to stand in his defense. Taking a public position in support of what's right, helping those in need, giving of yourself in service to your community—these are things of worth. Producing value in the lives of others helps a kid recognize his own value. Self-esteem follows from right actions.

Kids aren't dumb. If they've screwed up, they know it. No amount of self-esteem training will change their awareness of their own failures. Conversely, if they've done a great job and they know it, it doesn't matter who cheers them; they'll feel good about what they did because it has inherent value.

How does all this help your son's self-image? It's a matter of focus. Rather than talk about self-image, let's talk about self-respect, a far more effective way to get kids to like themselves. Teenage boys need to be good at something. It can be musically, intellectually, athletically, artistically, philosophically, scientifically. Your job is not to jam something down your boy's throat. Rather, be alert to opportunities where your son can shine.

Remember that self-respect comes from taking action. That means personal movement. Boys who spend too much time in front of the TV or computer screen don't have much chance to make a real difference in the world. Encourage your son to take some risks and chances, to discover what it's like to go farther than he thought he could go. Now *that's* living! Self-esteem respects who you are; self-respect honors what you can be!

When Teen Boys Lie

Shading the truth, misrepresenting the facts, not telling the full story. Your son fears reprisals for his disobedience, so he doctors his story a bit. It's time to face a simple truth: You're being lied to, and there is very little you can do about it. Some parents find out about lies firsthand; the rest of us have to just assume it to be true.

Think back to your own teen years. How many things did you do that would have turned your parents' hair gray if they had known? And now that their hair has turned gray naturally, how many of your teen exploits are still a secret from them? I was a pretty good kid and don't remember giving my parents that much trouble. But I kept a lot of things secret. If that was true of me, a basically solid-citizen type of teenager, imagine the lies that were told by the bad boys!

Now that we've established the universality of teens not always telling the truth, what are parents to do about it? I suggest you handle lying like you handle everything else: head-on and with surprising frankness. Start a conversation with your son on the spur of the moment, for no particular reason. Encourage him in a fun, playful way to admit he has secrets and has told you lies. He may deny that he's ever done so, but encourage him to come out with it. Tell him you're not going to bite his head off for being human. If you can get him to do that, you'll be inside his head in a way that few parents ever experience.

Then settle a deal with him: He can have his secrets (which he'll do anyway) as long as he keeps you up to speed on the important stuff. Discuss what the important things are: drugs, illegal stuff, girls, his whereabouts, nighttime plans, any threat to his health and safety, ideas about seeking employment, serious plans about the future. Let him know you're willing to give him some leeway in a few areas, but there are some issues that you insist on flat-out honesty.

This is also a good place to express to your son how difficult it is to give him good advice when you only have some of the information, or when lying has destroyed the trust between you. Express what it feels like to be lied to—not from the moral/spiritual angle, but from the personal "it makes me feel like…" angle. That's very hard for him to get defensive about and might actually smoke him out of his hideouts. Reiterate that trust is earned, and that you wish for him to be wealthy in trust.

Early Teens, the Tough Years

Boys between the ages of twelve and fourteen truly do represent the tough years for parents. I get more mail from parents of teens in this age range than all the others combined. It's no wonder. I read a report not long ago citing interviews with graduating high school seniors. They were asked: "At what age in your school years were most of your core values, beliefs, and bad habits created?" The overwhelming majority said the junior high years.

Those of us with junior high schoolers know the tangle of emotion, immaturity, irritability, instability, and susceptibility to peers that mark these volatile years. You probably also know the intense frustration of trying to work with these kids. They're not quite kids anymore, but they're not adults either. They don't respond like kids, but they're way too immature to be approached as adults.

So what should you do? I'd suggest several things. First, use this time to build your ability to be patient. There is little you can do about the nonsense that tends to flood out of these kids, so don't let it ruin you. You know some of the craziness: One minute they act like mature adults, the next total idiots; one minute they use great judgment, and the next they do something that nearly gets them killed. Roll with this kind of unpredictable chaos and exercise some patience.

Second, remember that your boys will climb out of this morass of confusion quickly, and you don't know when it will come. But be on the lookout. You can expect flashes of maturity where they'll talk sensibly and be generally agreeable to deal with. Look forward to these episodes. If all else fails, you can pretty much expect that the senior high school years will mature them almost overnight, so be patient.

Third, if possible, get your son in the presence of older guys. All junior high school boys want to be accepted and hang with the older guys. They'll do most anything to enjoy that privilege, including curbing their idiotic early adolescent high jinks. So if you have older teen nephews, sons, or friends in the neighborhood who are good examples for your son, try to get them together. A little positive modeling will go a long way.

Career Choices

I've been mildly obsessed with the matter of career choices for several years. I have kids growing up in a time of unbelievably rapid and hard-to-grasp change. I want to wisely advise my daughter and sons as to what career paths to explore, but it's exceptionally tough when the work world is in such flux. So I read as much as I can and then try to predict what their world might look like after college.

The world as we know it is rapidly coming to an end, and I don't mean in the biblical sense. If the current rate of technological advancement continues, computers will be practically indistinguishable from humans in about twenty years. Most of the actual work will be done by machines. Most of the work force will have to be continually trained and retrained for new careers that nobody has even heard of yet. We'll all change careers many times before retirement age. And all this will arrive at the same time our sons will be raising children of their own and making their mark in the work world. The challenges this will present to the work force will be nothing short of dizzying. How shall we prepare our sons to thrive in this yet unseen world?

The starting place is to prepare them to get basic education, then advanced education, and then to prepare them to keep learning for the rest of their lives. Education will be the dominant industry of this millennium, as our knowledge-based economy expands to include every field of endeavor and every working person.

If we want jobs in the future, we have to learn to do things computers can't do. It's also more important than ever to do things you love to do. Competition will remain stiff for the best jobs. So get your kids ready to work hard, achieve, and excel at whatever they are talented in. Impress upon them the value of competing well and winning. It's time to equip our kids for the coming changes.

Explain to them the importance of finding joy and passion in their work. This is more important than ever before because people not committed to the direction they're going will be forced to serve those who are. And that's no fun. Unfortunately, too many kids have no idea what they want to do—what they're passionate about.

Anthony Robbins uses a technique I like for helping your kids (and yourself, for that matter) define what they're passionate about. He suggests creating the job you hate. List all the things you would hate to do. Many kids will find this an easy list to make. Owing to their rebellious natures, they're far more familiar with what they don't like than with what they do like. Make the list as detailed as possible. Then Robbins suggests reading over the list. As you do, notice the feeling of strong revulsion or discomfort about the job requirements you would hate. That's passion, he says.

Now turn it around. With that "passion" flaming within you, write the list of things you would dearly love to do. Against the backdrop of the things you passionately dislike, create a detailed list of jobs and work activities that you feel strongly, and positively, passionate about.

Do this with your kids and begin the process of determining a future career. This is one of the most important parental responsibilities you have. Your son's career will change many times over the course of his life, but the time you spend with him now will be invaluable as he makes future decisions based on social factors, technology, and economic situations that we can only dimly envision. Preparing our sons now is like sending them off to the future with a bag lunch to keep in their backpack for when they get hungry. Pack it well...they'll need it.

Chapter Eighteen

Answers to the Big, Troublesome Teenage Issues

Violence, suicide, the occult, homosexuality, and other problems

This chapter requires a bit of an explanation. I generally receive three kinds of e-mail from the parents of teen boys. The first category of questions comes from people who are, in my opinion, just curious to see if they can get an author to write back. They're "fans" in the loosest sense of the word. Second are ordinary parents with typical problems. These folks are facing the trying challenges of raising perfectly normal teen sons. Then there are those parents who have a really serious situation on their hands, and they desperately need some reliable input. These problems always prompt me to think, sometimes for days, before I reply.

If it were me dealing with a son in some of these situations, I'd be wetting my pants. These are the *real* toughies, the hard situations that don't appear to have a good solution. I'll give you my best take, recognizing that some things that happen to us are beyond definitive answers.

Having said that, I hope the following advice will provide some useful guidance and clear direction.

When we talk about teenage boys struggling with really serious problems, keep in mind that most kids operate on the basis of a very simple system: Keep pushing until someone stops you. Then, when stopped, push some more. This system is powerful because it's effective. Some teenagers push like this because they've discovered it works; the other person backs down. Pushing allows the teen to get his way, even when his desired course of action is immoral, illegal, or self-destructive.

Take heed. Backing down in the face of disrespect or uncooperativeness sends the wrong message. Far better to cure the situation. In society, lawlessness is tolerated until it isn't tolerated anymore. The same is true in your home. You must draw the line and refuse to budge. I'm saying this so dogmatically because I don't want you to fall into a common parenting pitfall, that of making excuses. When you make excuses or assign blame, you stop thinking. And times of trouble are no time to stop thinking! Blaming or making excuses sends the wrong message. It's much better to stay on your feet, try to relax, and think clearly. I hope the following answers will help you do these things and more.

The Occult

The spiritual realm of darkness, the influence of paganism, the allure of the occult. These things alarm most parents, and rightfully so. Scripture tells us that spiritual warfare is real and should be taken seriously. We don't want our teenage sons to put themselves in a position of falling prey to spiritual deception.

But how much experimentation with the occult is a rejection of our faith, and how much of it is simple curiosity? Teenagers are interested in everything, and in their minds the weirder the better. Interest in the occult often fits into that domain. But if your son has adopted the symbols of witchcraft or paganism, is fascinated with the idea of contacting the spirit world, and has little use for the church, what should you do?

Remember that a periodic fascination with the weirder dimensions of our universe isn't all that abnormal. Sometimes it's a fleeting interest: pentagrams today, NASCAR racing tomorrow. It's a steadfast, continued fascination with the occult that presents a serious problem. The kids who get involved in these things almost always feel alienated from their peers and society in general. They are seeking camaraderie, acceptance, and a place to fit in. Their interest is not really in worshiping Satan or communing with the dead. They are interested in finding a group that will embrace them without judging them. The avoidance of rejection and the hunger for acceptance are strong motivating factors in any teen's life.

You can help fix this situation by initiating a dialogue. Talk to your son about what you have noticed and let him know you want to find out why he is pursuing this interest. Try not to become too alarmed. One of the psychological mechanics that keeps private occult practices going is your son's belief that you'd freak out if you knew what was going on. (Teenage boys love to get a rise out of the old folks.) Simply put, your refusal to become alarmed takes some of the fun out of it. This should be enough to remove the mystique and appeal for many of what I would call "garden-variety" occult fascinations of teenage boys.

Then of course there are the hard-core guys. If your son's fascination doesn't end quickly, follow this rule: Do what you can. You can't completely control your son's life, but you can control a great deal. You own the house he lives in, so enforce some rules. Don't allow posters, jewelry, symbols, amulets, fetishes, demonic figurines, and the like into your home. Make it clear that if you find these things, they will be destroyed.

And of course, as if you need to be told, pray for him. Teenagers are very spiritually conscious and open to the acceptance of unseen forces. This is a great avenue in which the Holy Spirit can work, and praying has and will continue to do miraculous things. Just keep believing that your son will be one of the really intriguing and happy turnaround stories that we love to hear about. Even with the hard-core kids, most of this occult fascination will burn out eventually. Occult things are just too weird for most boys to cling to for very long.

After pursuing false spirituality, many kids are left even more hungry for God's truth. If your son is younger, try to get him involved in the many youth-oriented outreach programs such as Young Life, Fellowship of Christian Athletes, Youth for Christ, Awanas (for much younger kids), and the like. Early intervention is always the best solution.

The Threat of Suicide

Nothing strikes fear in a parent's heart like the thought that a child is so distraught that he might take his own life. Teenagers feel things deeply. Their emotions soar much higher, and drop to more extreme depths, than the emotions of adults. And this seesaw of feelings can rise and plunge many times in the same day. There's no pattern, no order, no clear cause-and-effect relationship.

"I'd be better off dead!" Is that simply the angry utterance of a hurting teen or an indication of a serious contemplation of death? No matter how much a teenager has thought about ending his own life, suicide is always an act of impulse. Even with kids who seem to plan it out ahead of time, arranging all the details and even leaving a note, the act itself boils down to a snap decision.

Follow the local newspaper, and you'll notice that suicides tend to run in waves. Silly as it sounds, kids many times kill themselves because someone else has. Circumstances converge in a certain way, and the teen decides now is the time. After all, another kid at school did this same thing just last week.

Given the high incidence of teen suicide and the volatility of kids' emotions, let's take a look at what is going on inside the head of suicidal kids. A teenager's deepest need is for familiarity. They might resort to killing themselves because they feel alone and hopeless—lost in completely unfamiliar territory. The biggest threat arises when teenagers see their problems as permanently unchanging. Adults know that few things are unchanging, and in fact life can change for the good in an instant. But teenagers don't always have enough life experience to know things can get better, and they have an inborn, immature tendency to think that what's happening right this instant is what's going to be happening forever.

With that in mind, there are several ways a parent can help prevent this tragedy. The best way to fight suicide risk is to raise kids to have hope even in seemingly hopeless circumstances. Talk about the future honestly: As a long journey with lots of turns, unforeseeable problems, and unexpected opportunities, there is *always* hope for a better tomorrow. Kids with such a long-range vision would never resort to killing themselves.

Second, help your kids do something of powerful meaning to them. When a kid likes his life, he doesn't want to leave it. When you help your son develop a talent, skill, or hobby of great personal pride, you give him something he will keep forever. Don't force your agenda on him. Rather, spend time finding out what he likes and wants to achieve. Kids whose parents help them achieve their own personal goals are very happy kids.

Third, help your teen seek meaning in places other than his looks, his grades, his popularity, and his life circumstances. A teenager must learn that although life is disappointing and his talents and skills are limited, he can still make good things happen. He can use his strong desires to create a life that comes closer to matching his goals. Kids armed with this attitude will always search for answers and create solutions as they need them.

Of course, if your son has already attempted suicide, get him some professional help. Try to find a younger therapist with a strong personality and a good attitude. Seek out someone who can approach your son as an assistant and friend, not as a detached professional or know-it-all authority figure with some funky therapist's couch.

Violence and Intimidation

Some kids believe that the best way to get people to cooperate is to mistreat, threaten, and physically intimidate them. I refer to these teens as having only one speed in a five-speed world. Violent and intimidating teenagers have failed to learn better ways of getting what they want. Never forget that behavior is a tool for getting what you want, and the greater variety of behaviors you can master, the more results you are capable of achieving.

Violent teenagers need to expand themselves by developing broader skills and competencies. And until they do, you should never tolerate violence. It is never *ever* your responsibility to allow anyone to rule you with threats. And don't use spirituality as an excuse. Too often parents try to convince me that it's God's will that they live with abusive kids in the name of "love and long-suffering." God doesn't will that one person be abused by another person. Not in my home, and not in yours.

You do your son no favors by allowing his rampant, unchecked nastiness. You do him a much greater, loving service to help bring him to a place where change is possible. If your teen is not responding by becoming kinder and more cooperative under your care, then you're not helping him learn to succeed in life.

Kids who resort to violence keep at it because it gets them what they want. If you're not able to resist their pressure, you'll need to move them out of your home to another environment so they can restart the learning process. For a list of resources that will direct you to the help you and your son need, check my Web site at www.beausay.com.

Questions About Homosexuality

A teenager's sexuality is of great concern to parents. If he's dating, we want him to treat his girlfriend with respect and not view her as a sex object. We hope for sexual "normalness" for our sons and, with that, a clear sense of the dignity of women, self-respect, and self-control.

Ironically, many parents also fear the opposite. If a boy isn't panting after some girl, we worry that he doesn't have a "natural" sex drive. If he hasn't dated in a while, we might secretly fear he's got a sexual problem. If we never bust him for having a copy of *Playboy* hidden under his mattress, we don't know whether to be relieved or concerned. A kid with his sexual urges under control is one thing, but a son with no raging interest in girls is mildly worrisome, too.

Homosexuality is an extremely hot topic. Does a homosexual tendency automatically lead to a practicing homosexual lifestyle? With more boys being raised by single mothers, will we be seeing a higher percentage of boys who prefer the romantic company of other males? And with gay rights and sexual lifestyle issues getting so much press, the question of homosexuality ranks high on the list of concerns and questions on the minds of teenage boys. If a kid feels a funny tingle when he's showering with other guys after gym class, does it mean he's destined for a life of homosexuality?

Due to the highly charged nature of this conversation, I pray that we can all keep in mind that we love our sons deeply, no matter what choices they make. They'll make many decisions we won't approve of, but we'll still accept them. That's part of what it means to love our kids. So apply that same level of tolerance and unconditional love to the question of homosexuality.

Most of the gay men I've quizzed about their lifestyle tell me that their homosexual identity began forming early in their teen years. This makes sense, because that's when sexual awakenings occur. Hormones are raging, and a teenage boy can get an erection simply by squirming in algebra class. Sexuality is a tremendously powerful and overwhelming mystery that overcomes teen boys constantly and produces countless questions. Since erections and sensations and passions and erections and more erections seem to come out of nowhere, questions about sexual orientation are bound to cross a kid's mind!

When I talk to gay men, most have told me that they always knew they were gay. And even though they didn't like it, they felt they were somehow wired that way. Like being left-handed or gifted in music, these men just felt an unexplained attraction to other males. It had little to do with being raised by a single mom or having been molested as a child or any of the typical reasons people come up with to explain it. Most of them just had this feeling. They tried to fight their inclination by seeking to identify with heterosexual men. But eventually the facade became too heavy to bear, so they "gave in" to the lifestyle. Ask one hundred gay men how their lifestyle started, and you'll almost always hear some version of this story.

Statistically speaking, almost every teenage boy wonders at some point whether he's homosexual. Teen boys ponder this question because of the stage of life they're in. They wonder about *everything*. Most teenage boys, while wishing to be as "normal" as everyone else, sometimes catch themselves doing "not-normal" things. They might look at another guy's body with admiration or envy, wishing to have the same build or powerful muscles as the other guy. Or a teen boy might sense a greater comfort level when he's around guys, realizing it's much easier to talk to other boys—joking, telling stories, understanding one another. Girls, on the other hand, are much more complex and harder to understand. Does that mean he prefers guys over girls?

Some teen boys catch themselves having strangely affectionate feelings toward another guy. Is it simply deep friendship, or does it cross the line into romantic attraction? To a young, immature mind, these feelings and questions aren't easy to sort out. A teenage boy doesn't have the life experience to sort out momentary impulses from a full-on sexual orientation.

If your son fears he's gay because he's had occasional homosexual thoughts or even homosexual contact of some type, he'll probably never mention it to you. The word *homosexual* strikes terror in the heart of most young guys, so when they find themselves skirting along the edges of feelings and impulses that would fall into that category, they'll clam right up. The best thing you can do is to initiate an open dialogue about sex (which is good and deeply helpful among parents and teens), and simply express that homosexual feelings are normal and fleeting for most boys, and that such feelings certainly don't make a person gay. Again, surprisingly frank and reassuring comments on your part go a long way.

But what if your son is a practicing homosexual? Was he born this way, or is it a learned behavior? No one really knows the cause. I don't know, and frankly I don't care. I do care about people, teenagers included, controlling themselves and calling themselves to a higher plateau of personal excellence. I think all kids should strive for things that are out of reach and learn what it means to work and endure pain and privation to achieve difficult things. Too many men give up and give in to homosexuality when such surrender is avoidable. We need to teach all of our kids, homosexual or not, to strive for the higher things.

Loving your son is another matter. God loves us either way. He loves homosexuals, and you should too. I heard Billy Graham interviewed by Larry King one night. King was really pinning him down on a variety of controversial topics. Billy Graham, ever the sincere and kind man that he is, was asked if he'd love his son if he committed adultery or murdered someone. Billy Graham said of course he'd still love him. Then King pulled out the bazooka: What if your son came home and told you he was gay? Billy Graham thought a moment and said, "Though I wouldn't agree with his choice, I would love him all the more for it."

If you are the parent of a homosexual son, love him with everything that you have and then let God take care of the rest. That's the final word.

Heartbreakers and Underachievers

I am often asked about boys not working up to their potential. This concerns parents of sons who are lazy or unmotivated and also the parents of boys who have some unusual gifting that Mom and Dad really want him to develop. It's not unusual for a brilliant son to leave his schoolwork untouched; the natural athlete to quit the basketball team; the virtuoso musician to take a dislike to the band teacher and ditch his musical training. This is a touchy issue that requires wisdom and patience on your part.

Before we explore this matter, let's get something on the table. No matter how gifted your son is, he will disappoint you by failing to fulfill his potential at some point in his life. That's because disappointment and heartbreak stem from what *you* expect from your son. In effect, you create your own heartbreak when your son fails to perform up to your standards. Your boy probably has different ideas and plans for his life, and you're foolish to ignore this discrepancy.

To the extent you can, become familiar with what your son expects from himself. Try to understand how he judges his own gifts and talents (physical, intellectual, athletic, creative, artistic) and what he thinks he has to offer to the world. Don't be surprised if what he sees for himself fails to align with what you see as his strong points. Keep telling yourself, "This is his life to live, not mine."

Taking such a hands-off approach is not easy. It's especially hard if your son has some exceptional gifting in areas that you admire. Try to avoid shoving your preferences on him. Let him choose. Nobody can outrun his own gifting, and though he may not act on his gifts now, the gift will tantalize and tempt him for the rest of his life. In time he will make his own decision about which of his gifts he'll develop and which he'll keep on the mantel to look at from time to time.

Hard as it may be, your job is to support and encourage your son. Don't blame him for doing what his heart tells him. You did the same when you were his age.

Spiritual Renegades

I often receive e-mail from parents who are distraught over the spiritual condition of their teen boys. The saddest thing about this is that, as parents, we might bear some responsibility for a son's lack of spiritual fervor. In some ways we have done a poor job of making God an attractive option for our kids.

The reason is twofold. First, many of us are inconsistent in bringing God into our own lives on a daily basis. You can't tell bright, inquisitive hypocrisy-detectors (teenagers) to trust God and then sit around worrying about the electric bill. Like it or not, they see a lack of faith and learn one of two lessons: Either your faith is hollow, or your God is a wimp. A parent's consistent Christian life is the most powerful testimony of God's reality to a skeptical teenager.

Second, remember that kids gain part of their identity through rebellion. You say right, they say left. You say quiet, they say loud. You say God, they say "no way." They define themselves by pushing away from you. They separate from you so they can get a clearer look at who they really are. Sometimes the process of defining their own identity begins with clarifying who they are not. And that begins with not being the same as their parents.

Be patient with your son. Look past his rebellion and peer deeper. You can never know someone by his rebellion—what he's striving *against*. You can really only know someone by understanding what attracts him—what he's striving *for*. In the heart of all rebellion is a deep yearning for something, and if you care about your son, that's where you'll focus your effort. Don't fight the rebellion, explore it.

Remember that deep inside your teen lies something special—a native, inborn curiosity about spiritual matters. You have to learn to feed this curiosity like you'd gently fan tiny embers that you want to catch fire. You carefully tend young fires and build them up gradually. Likewise, explore where your rebellious son is headed in life and be patient.

Allow me to add a final thought. Faith is a funny thing: You can't make your son buy into it. He must choose for himself. He must feel the hunger and desire for God firsthand; otherwise he's just a cute little boy in an uncomfortable necktie reciting Bible verses, and feeling nothing. I was like that for a long time.

If you have a real passion for seeing your son achieve Christlikeness and openness to spiritual matters, make room for him to find that hunger within himself. Be careful not to force-feed God to your son, for that can sometimes backfire badly. Rather, let him suffer the spiritual pangs and longings for himself. Pain and misery aren't bad things if they motivate the right action. Rather than chasing your son to cram spiritual nourishment down his unwilling throat, leave a feast out in the open and let him come and eat when he gets hungry. Make him feel welcome at any time.

He'll get hungry. They all do.

Index

About the Author

Bill Beausay conducts seminars, workshops, and speeches nationwide. His newest seminar is titled "Smarter, Tougher, Wiser: Twelve Street-Smart Ways to Build Incredible Teens."

To obtain information about Bill's "encounter workshops" that bring teens and parents together for an unforgettable evening of life-changing interaction, or to learn more about other aspects of Bill's work,

check his Web site at
www.beausay.com

or call him at
(225)262-6229

or write to him at
P.O. Box 78383
Baton Rouge, LA 70837

or e-mail him at bill@beausay.com or bbeausay@aol.com.